INSANE!

Psych
thriller

# IN THE REALMS
# OF THE UNREAL

## "INSANE" WRITINGS

# IN THE REALMS
# OF THE UNREAL

## "INSANE" WRITINGS

COMPILED AND EDITED BY
JOHN G. H. OAKES
WITH DONALD KENNISON

**FOUR WALLS EIGHT WINDOWS**
NEW YORK

Published by:
Four Walls Eight Windows
PO Box 548
Village Station
New York, N.Y., 10014

First edition.
First printing April 1991.

Library of Congress Cataloging-in-Publication Data:
In the realms of the unreal: insane writings / compiled and edited by
John G. H. Oakes.—1st ed.
    p.        cm.
ISBN: 0-941423-52-2 (cloth)/ISBN: 0-941423-57-3 (paper)
    1. Mentally ill, Writings of the.   2. Mental illness—Literary collections.
I. Oakes, John G. H.
   PN6071.M415  1991
   808.8'9920824—dc 20                    90-27390
                                                   CIP

Text designed by Cindy LaBreacht

Printed in the U.S.A.

THE IMPETUS for this book came from another Four Walls Eight Windows title, *Asphyxiating Culture*, by the French artist Jean Dubuffet. Dubuffet there takes a proudly independent stand, arguing for a culture that reveres spontaneity and genuineness, as opposed to the carefully schooled work of a mythic Academy. Editing that fierce, but somehow naïve manifesto, it occurred to me that Dubuffet's comments, which to date have been formally applied only to the visual arts, were applicable to the written word as well.

In *Asphyxiating Culture*, which parallels the related work of German artist and thinker Joseph Beuys, Dubuffet exults in individuality. "Where is your normal man?" he writes. "Show him to me!" In his home, he founded the *Musée d'art brut*, now in Lausanne, Switzerland, dedicated to showing the work of "Outsiders"—a word coined by Roger Cardinal, which well indicates the direction of Dubuffet's interest.

Dubuffet can be accused of naïveté for his emphasis on the powers of individualism: one has only to note the almost obscene appropriation of the works of such "Outsider" artists as Martin Ramirez, Henry Darger and many others to realize that a new aesthetic, and consequently, a new Academy, simply imposes itself, and that the rich, anarchic chaos Dubuffet dreamt of cannot come to pass as long as the market economy rules. As Roger Cardinal observed, collectors who once were fascinated with "Tribal Art"—so-called "Primitive" works—now are turning their attentions to the next most easily exploitable area, that of the "Outsiders." Already, lithographs of some of the leading "Outsider" artists are available in editions of one hundred—a fact that is neither good nor bad, but to my mind one that would seem to obviate their existence as work "outside" the moneyed, commercial world.

Surely because the dollars available to the literary world are so vastly fewer, on the average, than those exchanged in the auction houses and galleries, the writings of "Outsiders" have been neglected. Yet just as many of the paintings of, say, Adolf Wölfli seduce the viewer—with their irreverence, their function as pure vehicles for Wölfli's imagination, as opposed to works done to order or even works done with the prevailing fashions in mind— Wölfli's writings are equally compelling, even when transcribed into cold type, even when translated.

Reading through this anthology, it is hard not to be reminded of the work of some of the most notable writers of the century— Samuel Beckett, William Burroughs, Franz Kafka, the Language Poets . . . And there are examples of writings that seem to bear no relation to preceding or contemporary works.

The prose and poetry chosen here were selected from among as many sources as I could contact, given limits of time and energy. No doubt the anthology leaves out poems and stories that should have been included. I hope that this book—the first of its kind in English—will inspire other anthologies of a similar nature. An effort was made to include a wide variety of authors: living and dead, free and institutionalized, foreign and American, contemporary and antique. By and large, the work in *In the Realms of the Unreal* has never before been published. Almost none has appeared in English. And some of the better-known names left out of this book, like Christopher Smart or Antonin Artaud, I and Don Kennison judged would have been out of place in an anthology that is directed towards presenting new work—meaning work that has not been widely read, if read at all. Furthermore, Artaud is considered a professional writer—someone who made (or attempted to make) a career out of the written word. That was the major argument against inclusion of his works, at least for the purposes of this collection. One might raise the same point against Mary MacLane, but MacLane's work was never accepted into the literary canon. She had the double strike against her of being a woman and an eccentric during a period when society was particularly oppressive and unforgiving.

We were looking for unusual poems and stories, often by people who had been or were currently institutionalized—although someone like Henry Darger (whose epic text lent its title to this volume) to our knowledge was never treated for "mental illness." The amount of material produced by these unusual thinkers has greatly diminished in the modern era, principally because of the use of psychiatric drugs that often dull creativity, even as they help a patient adjust to life in conventional society.

No common theme to the book should readily emerge. To again borrow a phrase of Roger Cardinal's, we are exploring an archipelago of ideas, rather than a continent.

The general sympathies of *In the Realms of the Unreal* should be conveyed by the subtitle suggested by Bolek Greczynski, coordinator of "The Living Museum" at Creedmoor Psychiatric Center: *"Insane" Writings.* The concept of insanity is called into question and the emphasis is on the works themselves, not their creators. These writings are not presented as clues to someone's "illness": they are published for their intrinsic worth.

Were it not for Don Kennison, who devoted months to the sorting and transcribing of material, some of it written in pencil on tiny scraps of paper, and whose editorial input was invaluable to the selection of the poems and stories, *In the Realms of the Unreal* would never have seen print.

From the field: many thanks go to Prof. Roger Cardinal; Bolek Greczynski and the patients who participate in Creedmoor's "Living Museum," who together changed my notion of the meaning of "mental illness;" Phyllis Kind; Valerie Koropatnick and the patients at Westview House; Cindy LaBreacht; Dr. Leo Navratil of the Gugging Institute; Laurie Parsons; Peter Rand; Karen Schechter of Creedmoor; Elka Spoerri of the Wölfli Foundation; and Dr. Michel Thévoz of the *Musée d'art brut*, whose book *Ecrits bruts* was indispensable to the formation of *In the Realms of the Unreal*. All whom I contacted generously provided much-needed advice.

To the translators—Roger Cardinal, Sophie Hawkes, Peter and Sarah B. Hoffmann, and Claudia Stoeffler—go my deep admiration for Herculean tasks extraordinarily well-done.

I would like to thank Carin Kuoni, whose skills as an artist and art critic were as important to the project as her experience as a friend. My parents, for their support in every sense of the word; my partner—co-publisher and friend—Dan Simon, for his quiet patience and persistence.

And to the many authors of this book, thank you for your forbearance: this anthology took over two years of research to put together, and I know that some of you despaired of it ever getting published. I hope you are pleased with the finished product.

JOHN G. H. OAKES
New York, January 1991

# FOREWORD

THERE WAS a time when clerical workers, if they were of a mind to, were allowed to put up funny or even impudent signs on walls near their desks, and such signs could be bought in what were then called "five and ten cent stores." One of these, I remember, was:

YOU DON'T HAVE TO BE CRAZY

TO WORK HERE,

BUT IT HELPS.

I may have seen that pre-fab joke for the first time at the Vonnegut Hardware Company in Indianapolis, where I used to work in the summertime in order to pay for clothes, dates, and petroleum. The store was owned by another branch of the family.

Then as now it was widely held that a person doing remarkably fresh work in the arts actually had to be crazy. What mentally healthy person could have thoughts that unusual? For a brief time, when my father was a boy, it was believed that there was a connection between tuberculosis and genius, since so many famous artists had TB. The early stages of syphilis were also rumored to be helpful. And E. B. White, the late writer and great editor of *The New Yorker,* said to me one time that he didn't know of any male author of quality who wasn't also a heavy drinker. And now, as though we needed any further proofs that creative persons are beneficiaries of disease, we have this volume of first-rate writings by the formerly or presently or since dead mentally ill, none of them, however, famous.

To me, though, and I have been in the writing business for a long time now, *In the Realms of the Unreal* proves only two things: first, that more good writing is being done than we can afford to publish and find time to read, and second, that creative people have thoughts unlike those of the general population because they have been culled or feel that they have been culled from that general population. The sequestering of some of us in mental hospitals is simply one of countless culling processes which are always going on. Tuberculosis or syphilis or a felony conviction or membership in a despised race or faction or a bad appearance or a rotten personality can get you culled as surely as a fancy nervous breakdown.

In order to be remarkably creative, though, it is not enough for a person to be culled or feel culled. He or she must also be gifted, as are all the contributors to this anthology. I have taught creative writing to all sorts of student bodies, ranging from those at Harvard University to teen-agers at a private school for the disturbed or learning disabled. I had thought that the percentage of persons with literary gifts is nearly the same for almost any sort of gathering. So why would that percentage, always a small one, be significantly higher or lower in a mental institution? Again: it is culling, whether real or illusory, rather than disease which is the source of inspiration. If it turns out that gifted people culled for mental illness have given the world more works of art worth saving than those culled for other reasons, that would make sense, since nobody can feel as steadily and alarmingly excluded from the general population. The rest of us make them the world's champions of loneliness. The word "egregious" (*outside the herd*) might have been coined for them.

As it is said: "Freedom's just another word for nothin' left to lose." There find encapsulated the benefit to a gifted person of being culled. Having nothing left to lose frees people to think their own thoughts, since there is no longer anything to be gained by echoing the thoughts of those around them. Hopelessness is the mother of Originality.

And the three lovely daughters of Originality in turn, the granddaughters of Hopelessness, as this volume demonstrates, are Hope, and the Gratitude of Others, and Unshakable Self-Respect.

KURT VONNEGUT
New York, February 1991

# TABLE OF CONTENTS

# UNITED STATES
# OF AMERICA

## THE QUEEN'S FOREBODING
*Intimations of Dementia / Gertrud's prebirth*

to let be or to not let be:
the prickly thorn of questing
all's too numb, dumbly askings
who's well who ends ill, before
issue of protests, portents and pretends;
'tis not of this world, this whelp
within my womb, knows where to prod
exactly on the tender foreknowledge
of vainglory's wonderings whamming
witchy whoo's owllike smuttings
besmirched within a belly's full
wailing already for the dark corridor
of entrance in and exit out, the re-
capitulation, nights' capricious giving-
in to the throne's dementia and demands
for princely conduct toward an ill-
defined need of hairy whooze and heir-
looms the size of pinpoints beginning
kingdoms-cometo loose this madness
on us all: God or gods befouled
by discordant desires and divine right,
whole destinies determined in the toss
of sickly seed, doubled by doldrums
(fishy and dunmarked) deeded rightly
and practiced nightly until this, now
a weighty waiting-in, thrashing within
an eternal doubt, deeped in a seeping
sac of unborn bones and hair and doom:

which way one turns, the lump is ever there,
and blood shall curdle on this moment's notice
of what has passed and shall yet pass
and crones know more than mother, while
mother wiles hours, as the obligatory ½
pleasure swells fullblown in the destiny
of bloody dust's insistence on his kingdom.

this alien madness crouching ready inme
kin of sodden saints worth but sick damns,
my profit no mere lamb, a sham seen slick,
with prophet's spoonfed ways, an offscene
stab in darkness, demon dancing on the edge
of bubbling tubs, stirring all the mucks
of aging sadness, growing forcefully to know
the mad why's of this his first decision:
letit go, let it be, Godbless,
and let him know the scrambly fixings
of one mother's obeying the obstructions
of queenly duty, you shall pay as you've
paid me, and kick and roll and moan
and madden, as my poor poor surrogate floats
down Lethe with pale flowers in her dead mouth.

APRIL–JULY 1987

RICHARD BEARD   "For the past 21 years I've been treated with a
number of medications and, it seems, an equal number of labels.
Presently I'm adjudged schizo-affective, and I willingly attend AA
besides. I wound up here in Portland in 1980, climbing off a Grey-
hound, in a mad fury, after over a year of sobriety, to have a few drinks,
and I never escaped (it's not a bad city!). I receive extensive counselling,
and manage to get by. While just another fool for love, I've not been in

it for 9 years. Originally I'm a New Hampshirite, attended Syracuse University, where I studied with Delmore Schwartz, among others."

## KELLY ROACH

### THE PLUMP WOMAN

Twenty to thirty pounds overweight
a plump woman
lieing on the bed nude
with a bent knee
a hand under her head
makes a pretty picture.

Flesh soft and smooth
skin warm and white
smells of cologne
fills the air
of romance and candle light
she becomes a pretty picture.

Saying in a soft harsh voice,
"Come to bed. . . ."
"come closer. . . ."
becoming a whisper,
this plump woman
makes a pretty picture.

The plump woman
is in love
with her husband
waiting for that special moment in bed,

saying from her heart,
"I love you. . . ."

KELLY ROACH  "I live in Hawaii. My present occupation is a retired writer. I've been a schizophrenic for 39 years."

## STEPHEN B. WYDE

### HE WAS STILL ALIVE

Some guys were sitting,
down at the day shelter,
waiting for the rain to die down,
after lunch, when one of them said,
"Hey, man, whatever happened to Joe?
I never see him down here anymore."
"I don't know," another answered him,
"But I haven't seen him either."
"I'll tell ya," a guy spoke up,
"I heard Joe died."
"Of what, man?"
"Cancer or the winter, I b'lieve.
They found him in the park,
all real thin and frozen up."
"No kiddin'," Ron said.
He had been Joe's friend.
"I heard he'd been sick, in the hospital.
But this."
Ron got teary-eyed,
said how he surely would miss Joe's jokes,
the crazy way he walked,

how he'd get in somebody's face for a cigarette.
The worker saw Ron crying,
brought him a paper towel.
"What'll you miss most about him, Ron?"
the worker asked him.
"Well, man," Ron spoke up,
"That guy owed me ten bucks!"
Everybody laughed.
"Hey, guys, rain's let up."
Ron walked out into the spring breeze,
glad he was still alive.

1988

STEPHEN B. WYDE    "I am a Mental Health consumer living in St.
Louis County. Forty-years-old, I have been a 'mentally ill' person since
1968. I am an advocate of Mental Health issues, and am currently
employed as an administrator for the Self Help Center, a Mental
Health agency here in St. Louis."

# EUGENE BISSONNETTE

## BRIDE OF LIFE

I saw a nun walking.
Worn-out the woman trod
Head bowed in deference
To a suffering God.
Her love made dross
By stigmatic savior on a cross;
She stooped spellful in prayer:
A sardius jewel of loss.

A choir of unremitting prayer.
Salivagous and dead in life,
Her self-devotement born of trust;
In spirit now the savior's wife,
Wearing a wedding gown of dust.

1989

EUGENE BISSONNETTE "My grandparents came from Italy; and I was raised in their strong Catholic beliefs. The religion became as tangible as life itself; and my poem is a view of the blessings and suffering which walk together like light and darkness in a single shell - the body of a nun who walks in hope of the unseen and sees the real world as reflections of a more real heaven and hell."

## RICHARD G. LOVE

ANGER

A lot of people who are in the hospital as staff say that anger is to be talked out calmly, coolly and in normal tones at all times.

I say that doesn't work all the time.

As an example, when I was growing up, people liked to be mean to me, including my own brother, to make me mad so that they had a reason to beat me up. Even if I asked them to stop it or ignored them, told someone or got angry at them the way the hospitals and school teachers said, I'd still get beat up and laughed at.

What I'm trying to say is that controlling anger has its place. Sometimes you have to yell, scream, punch someone, even fist fight to get the point across.

Now if none of these efforts work, then it just isn't worth it.

1988

RICHARD G. LOVE "I was born on 11/22/65 in Denver Colorado.
Moved to Vermont while still a baby.
I've been in the mental health system as long as I can remember.
I've seen it all."

# DAVID WIKAR

## LET THE DEER IN THE CITY

After all the bombs have fell,
when all you can make of yourself is deep and personal
hell,
when the earth is scared and there is no cure,
when the lonely runners legs are broke, and there are
no spectators there to cheer and make his heart endure.
When hatred is something in which you have to fight
for and kill,
When love is thought of as weak and corny and is
something that makes you frightened scared and ill.

Then you will be asked to let the deer in the city
and they will walk on your cement and broken glass,
and their gentle child-like feet will bleed.

Yes, let the deer, who symbolize everything gentle,
child, woman, man, every leaf, every flower,
will walk to your cities and will die from all your
hopeless vibrations,

because you never listened to the earth's gentle
sigh and tiny tears as you scared her
with all your satanic cities,

I dare you, even now to let the deer in the city.

1989

DAVID WIKAR    "David Wikar grew up in Bennington, Vermont and
has also lived in Boston. He currently lives in Burlington, Vermont.
David is an avid reader. He is interested in Eastern religions, philosophy and music and has an especially strong interest in the music of
Bob Dylan."

# RICHARD P. BEEMAN

## COURT APPEARANCE

Shredded before the judge
He bowed like Hanoi's principal agent
With shackled fists raised in rage
Branded like cattle by love and life
Skewed in tatoos pressing thresholds
Of reptilian skin
Her wirey frame tortured by psychiatric insouciance
His hell-in-the-head burns like inspiration
Derailed with five-knuckle-fury
Broken like yesterdays horse ride
And with the final fetters of hospital loving
Fat-cat-do-gooders closing in
Like every psychiatric hero, He stood tall
And cried silently

RICHARD P. BEEMAN    "I'm an ex-patient, now consumer. I consider myself a survivor of mental illness, mental health treatment and peoples views of those we call 'schizophrenic.' I am currently assistant director of Survivors On Our Own, a grassroots self-help services and advocacy group in Phoenix, Az. I hope through poetry to express the inner strength and outrage of the mental health survivor, and the sometimes hopeless bravado of that stance."

## DAVID BERNATCHEZ

### NEVEREND

Young, wasting away,
Vannette would die;
her money would go to me,
never seen.
At a picnic, Vannette, next to
an uncle,
turned to me,
pale, frail, and faint.
She should stay with me, I thought,
She might live yet, I thought,
hoping against hope,
to fend off death.
Vannette, Vannette, once,
never again.
Parched maturity of a fading
yellow flower, near a
macadam road.
Spruce, Blue spruce,
gold tinted green,

stretching onward.
We live, yet would not.
What can happen?
We don't know.
Clouds to the sky,
Songs to the rain.

1989


DAVID BERNATCHEZ   "I was born April 30, 1955 in Windsor, Vt. I grew up on a farm in West Windsor, Vt. I went away to the Vershire High School, a private boarding school, in 1969 and graduated in 1973. I had developed paranoia during the high school years, succumbing to a nervous breakdown and staying at Vermont State Hospital in Waterbury, Vt. 1974 through July 26, 1976. I stayed in boarding homes until I began to work, then had rooms or apartments. After close to a year of fulltime work my employer went bankrupt, but I fell back on an inheritance from my parents. I began to write and wrote a book, which I gave up. Since then (the last five years) I've studied literature, especially poetry. I've published with the 'Poetry Society of Vermont' and 'Counterpoint' in Burlington, Vt."


## RALPH DOOLEY

I exist alone and only
I am I
Can anyone see
I am I
I see you
Eye to Eye

Can't know, Can see
I am I
I exist only and alone

---

What's Done
Can't be un-
What's lost
Can't be won
some play to win
Others not at all
What makes a sin
What is a virtue
do people call
All I can say
I hate you one and all
and I'll kill someday

---

My cat,
fat,
sat,
Watching
the bird
in The Tree

RALPH DOOLEY   "I was in the hospital sometime ago and have had difficulty holding a job, but I am going to school now studying Business Management. I hope and I feel I will have my own business someday. P.S. poems 1 & 2 were written before the hospital, #3 recently."

## MIRIAM KALLUS

### A FAREWELL TO DARKNESS

I miss winter! We have longer days, more sunshine, buds are slowly bursting from our trees, but looking back on those long, cold and dreary winter days, where nothing was apt to be seen short of ice, I wish them here just once more!

I suppose I'm one of those bleary-eyed, drip psychotics, to whom nothing short of misery is pleasing . . . or maybe I even made a mistake by getting out of bed this morning? But whatever my feelings, for me, all things great and beautiful seem to be on the wane.

Spring! The unsightly site of it! Lake Champlain minus ice! Green everywhere mocking at winter's gray! Lengthening daylight! Putting away those favorite soggy wet boots! Warm breezes destroying my lust for cold!

What will become of me? Will I blow up in smoke? I'm at a loss . . . Oh well, (as the song says), "It might as well be Spring."

MIRIAM KALLUS    "Miriam Kallus was born in New York City after WWII and was raised in the city. She attended public schools and then college at Brandeis University.

"Miriam spent most of her twenties in Boston, teaching music after graduation. She was married briefly at age thirty and divorced a year later. Since then, she has been single and living in Vermont. Her hobbies are music, reading and painting."

## LIMITS

All of modern day Mathematical Calculus is based on a certain principle known as the "Central Limit Theorm." And lots of our technological culture depends on this "Calculus."

Individuals learn to expect certain limits to always hold true. Human communication also encounters limits. Some are arbitrary and some are forced. There are some subtle limits about interpersonal expression. Within given group settings, within given situations, limits take varying shape. We also think of limits as opposing our own physical activities. And also, the "mental patient" has found real forces in society trying to get him or her to limit their own brand of acceptable thinking activities.

Limits mean safety. Ask any in-training tightrope walker to try and deny this. But, I feel strongly, that having "no limits" does not imply "having no safety." A couple weeks ago I was asked by Odd Jobs to do a moving job, to help out in a pinch. I did this job, but partly due to my handicap from a six-year old brain damage, struggling with 80-pound bedframes inside 100-degree staircases pushed me way past some limits. For awhile I felt funny, say for a week. Looking back now, I can sense I've become physically lots stronger. My earlier exercise plan called mostly for long walks; this kept raising the endurance I had, but didn't affect my overall capacity.

As I see it, limits are really begging to be tested, tested, and finally revised. So we grow and we can begin to reframe our own objectives and our perspectives. Even a poem or a song that asks people to stop and wonder, "Why does this make me feel strongly?"—even a poem can go a long way towards challenging the subtle limits we daily depend upon.

1988

JIM TRANOWSKI   "Jim is a native of Chicago. He was born in 1954, graduated college with a B.A. in the philosophy of interpersonal communications in 1984 and relocated to Vermont in the winter of 1987. He is a computer-programming engineer by training and trade, who has also been witness to 'both sides' of mental health. He is currently employed part time as an engineer while evolving into an interacting part of the culture as seen at Westview House."

## MARC ANDRE THIBERT

### FINEST SWORDSMEN OF FRANCE

Findness Sword Men of France
Wear Warrie of France Social Parties
They would train hour at time
Eighteen Hour a day - sword swipe
would be like Flash of lightening.
Thay could cut and apple in four way
in air
and also cut button off your shirt
with out you even knowing it.

It was art by itself.

### ABOUT MARCIE PET FLY

One day meet a fly name crazy.
She was very funny.
The fly make circles in the air.
It would do a back flip in my cool coffee.

And also would do nosedive in my Cheerios.
It was funny.

1988

MARC ANDRE THIBERT  "Marc Andre Thibert was born in Fitch-
burg, Massachusetts in 1951 but has lived most of his life in Vermont.
He has been involved in mental health programs in that state since
1969. He comes from a strong French Canadian background and has
over 250 relatives in Québec. Along with his love of writing, Marc
possesses a passionate interest and enthusiasm for European people
and cultures." (Courtesy Westview House)

## JOSEPH STERN

### SCHIZO

I'll be both.
Although I am loth
To think of
Abandoning all
Like the horse in its stall
As I call
The pheasants home to roost.
The pills give me a boost
Into another world;
'Though they twirl
My mind on a roller-coaster
Like burnt bread in a toaster.
As if the night-time glare
Of locked doors

Could reduce the effect
Of some manic doctor's ruthless stare.

1989

JOSEPH STERN   "I was born and raised in Riverdale, New York. I am forty years of age and earned a Bachelor's Degree from Columbia University in 1972. Over the past twenty years I have been hospitalized five times and spent two and one half years in the hospital, total."

## JAMES WALTER ROBEAR JR.

REALITY CHECK

When you hear a voice in your head do you often wonder if it could be something more than a thought? I know, for instance that growing up I had three little imps that spoke into my psychic ears.

These imps I met when I was six years old. Somewhere in my grandmother's woods they latched on to my back and began to speak to me. They weren't really evil, but they would do their best to play with me at all times. I began to trust them because I doubted myself. Instead of using my own intuition, I used theirs.

So, it wasn't until I was twenty-one that I found out that they were imps. I went to a psychic healer and they found these three little green nature spirits attached to my back and took them away. I had lost some companions and the voices went away.

Later on I was always asked if I heard voices and I always said no. I didn't like being called psychotic, it didn't apply, and what did it mean? They certainly didn't comprehend. They looked for a quick solution and drugged me. Then they would listen and nod their heads. When you spoke, they judged your words as a delusion to confirm their concepts.

I learned to investigate where a voice came from and decided that at times there were beings speaking to me. I also learned that I could creatively change thoughts into voices. Not that this is the truth of reality.

I'm a being that can sense with my mind and spirit to search for the truth. I've been through madness and value a normal life, but let us be open to other realms and consider it real. Can some clear mind comprehend the truth still?

1988

JAMES WALTER ROBEAR JR.   James Walter Robear, Jr., 28, died January 19, 1989 after a long illness. He was born in Burlington, September 4, 1960, and attended Rice Memorial High School and the University of Vermont. His interests included cross-country skiing, bicycle touring, and weaving. He was a member of Christ the King parish. (Courtesy Westview House)

# CHRISTINE PEMBERTON

Bottles on my father's shelf hold some power over me. I am fascinated by the smoke curls that drift across their shiny surfaces. I am frustrated because I can't roll up into those wicked shadows. I want to join their ranks but they stand firmly as a mass, unbeckoning. They react as a group. In their conformity an ugly insensitivity is accentuated. Looking to see what is sustained there in, I find a challenge which is less restrained, yet somber still. I try to turn their voluptuous bellies inside out to enter the Proustian world within. There is something clever about that darkness holding more than this moment in time. Perhaps it is a collage of past and future images, a superimposition that might reveal the fragility of my existence. But because I am infinitely larger than the specks of dust who celebrate a dance of time, I can only strain and pretend to join them.

In the first bottle I see a window is contained. The mysteries of the abysmal world through these panes I will never see. And yet I feel my presence in that dark room. A face I do not know is forced upon me there. The ambiguity of the experience simply holds me there. Like a thousand other moments I have seen in paintings and photographs, detachment becomes part of the pain of belonging. One's surroundings don't always answer back. Familiarity is denied. Nothing is understood in touch. Shafts of light strips are frayed. There are shells of consciousness accepting a desperate cubist imagination. There is warmth in this terror because death and life are one.

Here on my father's shelf I think I have found that underlying rhythm which unites the separate bodies who wait at a bus stop with tombstones. For the moment at least, I treasure the precarious rape of identity. I succumb to the humble power.

1988

CHRISTINE PEMBERTON    "Christie Pemberton was born in Rio de Janeiro, Brazil of American parents. She grew up in Manhattan and attended Syracuse University, Barnard College and the University of Vermont. In 1980 Christie moved to Burlington, Vermont. She has worked in various capacities for *The Westview News*. In January 1989 she gave birth to a son."

## HEALING POEMS BASED ON R.D. LAING

The following poems were written during a psychotic episode during which I believed I was the Buddha. The poems were based on the type of poetry found in R.D. Laing's book *Knots*. These poems were an exploration of the process of going crazy and a means of returning to health. They were written in February of 1984.

## THE ONLY THING WE HAVE TO FEAR
## IS FEAR ITSELF

I am afraid of something
I think I am afraid
I think I can't think
I can't think I'm afraid
I'm afraid of thinking
I was afraid and now I am afraid of thinking
I'm afraid to think how afraid I really am.

I'm afraid
I think I'm afraid
I think I can't think properly
If I can't think How can I think I can't think?
But
I can't help but think
I'm getting afraid of thinking
The more I get afraid the faster I think
Faster and faster
I have to think faster than my fear
I'm afraid to stop thinking fast
I'm going to stay awake and think fast

That way I can stay ahead of fear
So . . .
I stay awake and awake and awake.

I am aware
I am aware that I am aware
I am aware that I am aware that I am aware
I bear the weight of too much cognition.

I like you
I think I don't like you enough
So I try to like you more
But that's not enough either
So I try even harder to like you
I try harder and harder and harder
But all I do is like you.

I try
But I think I'm not trying hard enough
So I try harder
But that's not enough either
So I try harder
I keep trying harder and harder
And I keep thinking it's not enough
Really all I was doing to begin with is try
You know some people don't even try.

I am a self
I observe myself
Once I could observe only the world and not myself
Now I observe myself
I am both observer and observed now
I am self conscious.

I think
I think that I thought

I am thinking that I thought that I thought
I am thinking that I am thinking
I am thinking that I am thinking that I thought that I thought
I am thinking
I am repeating myself
I think I am repeating myself
I think I thought I was repeating myself
I am thinking that I thought that I thought I was repeating
   myself
I am repeating myself
I think I am repeating myself.

I think you hate me
You are thinking I am thinking you hate me
I am not sure
Do you hate me?
You really don't hate me?
I was sure you hated me.
What a relief

I remember
I am thinking I am remembering
Now I am remembering that I thought I was remembering
Or did I remember that I remembered
Oh yes remembering and thinking are the same thing
Remembering is a type of thinking
Isn't it?
Therefore I think that I thought that I thought that I thought
So what!

I am afraid you are mad at me.
You are thinking I am afraid you are mad at me
I am thinking you are thinking I am afraid you are mad at me
You are really going to get mad because you think I won't be
   afraid any more after you do get mad

You are really going to get mad
At least I think so
Maybe
No I really think so
There . . . you did get mad after all
To hell with you.
At least I'm not afraid anymore.

I am afraid you are mad again
You know that I know that if you really do get mad I won't be
   afraid
We all know the theory of this
At least I think so
No I really think so!
I'll get mad if you get mad again
But I am afraid to get mad at you
I insist that I will be mad if you get mad
Why will I get mad?
Because I have done nothing wrong to deserve your anger
That's the bottom line
No the bottom line is that we have ground rules and I have
   obeyed them.


GOING CRAZY

I try to find an answer to my psychological problem
I find one answer
I think it's not enough
So I try to find another answer
I find an answer and now I have two answers
But I think that's not enough either
So I try again
Then I have three answers

IN THE REALMS OF THE UNREAL ■

But that's not enough
So I try again
Harder and harder faster and faster
I go to philosophy but that's not enough
Then I go to religion
Believe it or not that's not enough
So . . .
I become the answer
But all I need to do is realize I'm okay.

ROBERT C. LOOMIS  "I am 45 years old and single. I have lived in
Vermont all of my life which makes me a 'Woodchuck' (slang for native
Vermonter). I grew up in southern Vermont (the 'banana belt') on a
poultry farm and attended local schools until I went to college at Tufts
University. I left Tufts in the Spring of my third year because of a
nervous breakdown. Eventually I graduated from a small school in
Vermont with a degree in psychology. At first I worked as a geriatric
social worker for nursing homes but, once again, I had to leave because
of emotional problems. In the 1970s I joined an employment training
program—one of the remnants of Lyndon Johnson's 'Great Society'—
and learned the craft of producing a small newspaper. Eventually I
used these skills to start a small newspaper of my own for the mentally
handicapped. It is called 'Counterpoint' and is distributed statewide
and, to some extent, nationally. 'Counterpoint' is entering its sixth year
of publication and has given some stability to my life—both finan-
cially and psychologically. I have been out of the mental health
system, now, for four years and feel I have become a stronger person for
having negotiated life on my own."

# HARVEY PECK

## JUST ANOTHER PSYCHOTIC AFTERNOON

While sitting on my couch
one cold wintry day
I saw through the wall
much to my dismay.

The sky was deep purple
as well as the air
and strangely enough
I really didn't care

There were millions of Black Drops
rising from the ground
and spiraling upward into the sky
counterclockwise into a perfect cone.

One green tree was growing on my front lawn
and I still wonder why.
Yet my mind still looks to that cone of drops
rising so far into the sky.

Why was it purple
and only one green tree,
as if raining skyward
so peaceful to see.

1988

HARVEY PECK  "I was born in Burlington, the oldest of seven children. I didn't finish High School, however I did get a G.E.D. scoring in the top 99%. I started an electrical construction business at the age of twenty three and it grew into a multi million dollar business within ten years. I have three children and was married for 19 years. Now I have given my life totally to Jesus through the intercession of His Blessed Mother, Mary."

**PAUL JASPER**

DREAM

Last night, about 3AM in the morning, I had an intense dream. It was a dream about numbers and crowds of people and it was also about time. The way time is related to numbers and to living.

It seemed that less than an eye-blink could be detected as a sign of life. We are aware down to the tiniest second of time of life changing and flowing and dancing, like the clocks that register one tenth of a second. A person could express something in literally the blink of an eyelash. A man could express, for example, a hesitation or doubt in so quick an inflection of his voice or a movement of his head, that, in order for the communication to be effective, the listener or recipient should be so sensitive so as to realize these subtlties.

To detect this in a great flow of words or in a great crowd of people could be very taxing to the mind. In fact, one might start to feel that a big wave of people was washing one way and then the other, and that the subtlties of feeling could leave you drowning, washing up this way and the other. Similarly, if the words were of a very great number, then to pick up a nuance, a tiny breath might be so taxing that the inward and outward flow of thousands, maybe millions of words would strain the mind to the point of cracking it completely.

Our words are like people. We live in big cities of the mind, surrounded by millions and billions of words as well as people.

We talk and react to words like the crowds on 34th street in Manhattan as they look at the big lightbulb clock register-levels in tenths of seconds. The crowds wash back and forth. Men and women, all races and levels of poverty and wealth, of beauty and ugliness. The numbers on the clock do a sinuous and sensual dance. The six changing to the seven; the seven rapidly adding a curved bottom and a rounded top to become an eight. This is energy. This is the destruction of time.

1989

PAUL JASPER   "Paul Jasper was born in Brooklyn, where he now lives. He has published in New Mexico and in California. This poem came to him almost entirely as a dream, and is the first poem of this type to be published by him. He is currently writing a play."


## SUSAN A. NAEYE

### SUSPENDED ANIMATION

through the mist
of my despair,
I see an open door,
I turn around
only to come face to face
with an open door,
I look about
the haze,
the haze filled vacuum
clutching my heart,

I drift,
floating on broken dreams,
broken promises,
no tomorrows await me,
through the mist,
I see an open door,
the same door greets me
as I advance at each threshold
of pain,
I turn around
and come face to face with an open door,
through the mist,
I step through one door
only to be welcomed by yet
another open door,
standing wide open,
I stare into a blank hollow
towering over me,
through the cavernous mist
each doorway beckons me,
I wander in and out
only to come face to face
with an open door
that leads back to the same
elusive mystery that lies
beyond each open door,
lost,
I am imprisoned
by my illusion
of what waits for me
on the other side of the door,
if only I could cross over

I WAS NOT MEANT TO EXIST IN THIS WORLD
I PLUMMET FROM THE HEAVENS
FROZEN IN UNDERGROUND ICEBERGS
I CANNOT FEEL MY TOES

When will the nightmare-nightmare-nightmare-oblivion-the
sound of your voice hurting me inside end?
My guts piled in the open--feast for the vultures that swoop and
peck and peck-gobble tiny bits of my flesh with their sharp
beaks--the sound of your voice, a whip that snaps
in my nightmare.

1989

SUSAN NAEYE    "I am currently enrolled at Harrisburg Area Community College in Pennsylvania and have had a love of writing since
the age of 15."

# SUSAN L. ROSE

there's pain inside me
I don't know why
has the great god Depression
come back to visit me again?
I hurt
I'm twisted

inside
like a dishrag wrung out

1989

---

I climbed upon a roof
to see the sky
so far above
there was a bright lightning
and a voice spoke to me
smile my child
for all is well
god is in his heaven
and peace is not far away
the lightning bugs flew
and scattered
the bright light shone
and I smiled

1989

---

in depression there is hell
there is the drive to die
to escape the pain of life
but a gentle loving man
accepting me and holding me
can change things around
it isn't easy
he had to put a lot of energy
   into me

but who else and where else
could I find the love
that saved me from myself?

1989

---

a thousand voices calling me
I cannot answer
sweet voices calling me
I cannot cry
purple doves calling softly
I cannot listen
a thousand people smiling
I cannot smile
please help me god
for I am incomplete
my brain has holes
where the mice have been chewing
please help me god
for I am incomplete

1989

---

delicate child
    whispering in the night
fallen angel
lightning butterfly
    fluttering in the wind
so fragile

so near to falling
so close
   and yet so far...
tiny torments
building up over time
the seething volcano
sealed with granite on top
the depths
   and allyways
garbage strewn about
conrete jungle
   of the mind
twisted steel
and rotting filth
stomach rolling
veins boiling
the blood flows forth
I vomit upon your dreams

1989

---

the angel Gabriel stood high
and mighty
above the trees
all in shining
   white
a golden sword in his
   right hand
a golden shield in his left
a face full of vengeance

raising the sword
he began to bring it down
   upon me
but I too was towering above
   the forest
an electric blue light
surrounded me
I raised my left arm
and with a silver-white flash
deflected his sword
and knocked him back
   on his ass

1989

SUSAN L. ROSE  "I was born the 18th of November in 1957 near the
Pacific Ocean. I have lived and traveled through wildernesses of plants,
animals, people and concrete. I love to read and write, to create in
colors of the rainbow, and to take care of my newborn daughter,
Diana."

# BARBARA WEEKES

NOT QUITE BORN

Small trembles shake me,
this as I thought I was
better. Peering ahead, moving
through fluid, I see my nails
have scratched the skull
of a baby floating, not quite born,
which hovers in place of my head.

## IMAGE

Dark forms move around me;
waiting for them to subside
a small blue fish
died.
It passed out of my mouth
with yellow and green sea grasses.
There is no where to hide
until this passes.

## DAVID'S PSALM

Reaching through the dark—spilling out.
I have hung up the phone
knowing she would not have lied to me—
a shock of truth with no bottom.
The room expands,
a night bird careens overhead and dips its wings—
I am worn down.
People everywhere testing and labeling each other
using hand signals and a plague of rhyming words—
double meanings at every turn.
I have failed to untangle
the skein of this massive public-secret.
Not real—she said never real—alarm spreads.
It has happened.
Clouds of insanity tumble through the sky;
locked in I walk a multi-layered road.
My arms are stripped of skin; I cradle them against me.
Ah, God—
stunned I move toward the inner room.
The Lord is my shepherd, I shall not want.

My bed stands in the corner.
He maketh me to lie down in green pastures—
he restoreth my soul.
Suddenly fear is everywhere
tugging in the permeating dark.
The bird circles; its wing brushes against my hair.
Yea, though I walk through the valley
of the shadow of death
I will fear no evil      I will fear no evil.
Clinging to life by repeating parts of a psalm
over and over, like a mantra:
the Lord is my shepherd      I will fear no evil.
It was never them;
it has all been made up from within me.
I sink to the bed.
He maketh me to lie down in green pastures;
I need rest, to sleep in the shadow—
perhaps tomorrow I will find a way to stand.
She would never have lied to me—
restoreth my soul      restoreth my soul.
Exhausted: falling into nightmares
fighting to stay awake, to shake free of them.
Desperate by an abyss, terror is loose:
walls move in, the bedstand shifts out of sight;
black fissures open beneath me again and again—
holes in the vault of heaven with no bottom, no direction.
In my extremity I turn to the source
and find myself in the valley of the shadow
of death.
Am I alone beside these turbulent waters?

Two years have passed; time has shaped me.
Sometimes I am in the fields

for I have found my fragile hope in man,
but the Lord is not my shepherd and I will always want.

BARBARA WEEKES   "Barbara Weekes is a New Yorker. She feels that
her ability to write poetry is a dark grace. Being the editor of the
Fountain House Quarterly rounds out her personal commitment to
write and to bring poetry into the lives of others."

# ALVIN WILSON

## THE LITTLE FIFTY FIRST PSALM

God,
This isn't antiques, literature, or schizophrenia.
Kill me.
Please kill me God.
And don't forgive my sins.

God,
I gossip inside
On who's going to hell
Or not.
I marked my initials on Liberty.

I'm a good man that
Everybody likes.
I'm gentle
And clever.
I tell poetry like
"I've had my hiney wiped by a niggermammy
And been raped twice in the Birmingham jail."
I tell stories to children

"Once upon a time when
My cat was taking a possum's nap, and"
And I've stayed straight.

God,
I do do do
Hate my guts.

O, Lord in heaven
O, Most Merciful
Slip me please
A clean shave
Or cancer.

ALVIN WILSON    "Alvin Wilson is forty-five years old; native of Ala-
bama; two degrees (English - education); 10-14 hospitalizations; skitso-
manicdepressive; disabled; former school teacher, social worker; interested in art; independent. He likes front porches with friends, and finds
writing pleasurable and essential."

## NICOL

### BY MY OWN HAND

I watched these
cold stiff fingers
reach in searching
the sacred edge
the sharp undoing
and I didn't struggle
against them
as a long thin line

appeared
above the throbbing
and the sweet red wine
spilled over
and mixed itself together
with the bitter
of salty tears
and once again I lay
in this frothy soup
never knowing
what's to come of it
because I was
unable to bear
the best of it

NICOL    "I am a client of the DeNardo Center for the chronically
mentally ill. I've lived in Fairbanks, Alaska 9 years."

## BETH GREENSPAN

## PRAYING TO THE GODS OF OFFICE CEILING SPRINKLERS ON JUNIPER STREET

I've got a headache THIS FUCKIN' BIG
And it's thanks to you, you, you, you, you
And me and none of your useless white pills
Is going to set me free.
Think of needles through pinched skin
With lead weights hanging off the tips.
Think of every body position known to humankind
And every time you move to try and get comfortable,

You've got a leech gripping to each muscle,
Sucking life-blood out, injecting painful poisons in
So that every step, every turn of the head
Is a spasm of muted agony
As you just try to pretend that nothing is going on.

So with that in mind,
Think of sitting in an office trying to work,
And the more you try, the further behind you fall
And the pain—remember the pain?
So as the leeches multiply on your neck,
You're just sitting and staring up at the ceiling
And you notice, like you do every once in a while,
The sprinkler above the desk
So you just sit and stare into this metal god
And you start praying and praying with all the strength
You have left and you're praying that it will start spraying
Now, now, now and all of the papers and useless clutter,
Including you melting away in your chair, will start to drown,
And the door is closed so no one knows,
And it just sounds like a waterfall and everyone loves waterfalls
So no one thinks much of it—it's just those middle of day
    dreams,
And you like waterfalls too, and to be frank, you couldn't give
    a shit
If you get washed away and die along with all the stuff
You tried to do. So the office becomes a human fish tank
With you and everything else just floating around in it,
Because the water's been coming for many hours now
And the sun is setting over the stone city
And in one final burst, the window explodes
And all the paper fishes, and human fishes (you), and filing
    cabinet fishes

Gush out into the frozen automobile air
And everything lands SPLAT! on the pavement and in the trash
   bin below
But suddenly you yell NO! NO! NO! NO! NO! 'cause not a single
   thing
Has happened and you're still just sitting there praying
With the leeches exhausting your soul and you're just staring
At that damn little grey god that doesn't act and you're thinking
"It's all over, Baby Blue." and then you leave.


## BETSY

We were in the restaurant.
The waiter hung around our table
Like a damp rag.
You weren't there, really.
You were cloud-like.
Your velvet black hair
Was the point
On which I focused—
Your eyes like China beads.
The moment was lost
In a swirl of plates
Landing on our table.
Chicken salad.

BETH GREENSPAN  "Beth Greenspan is a twenty-five year old stu-
dent-on-leave living in Haverford, Pennsylvania. She has completed
two years of college and would like to return to Temple University to
study English/Creative Writing. Currently, she is the Assistant
Coordinator of the National Mental Health Consumer Self-Help
Clearinghouse. She is also co-founder of a small literary magazine.

Beth has been writing since the age of eleven, and she is an avid reader and has a collection of books numbering in the thousands. She enjoys playing guitar, listening to a wide variety of music, juggling, playing volleyball, watching movies, finding different ways of viewing and hearing the world, riding trains, attending and participating in poetry readings, observing and thinking about nature, late night reading and writing, and the first cup of good coffee in the morning. Beth has been a psychiatric survivor and 'system inmate' for about twelve years."

## SANDIE WOOD

YOU ARE SOMEBODY

You are somebody and have always been
And to think otherwise would be a sin
For the Lord our God in His Master Plan
Did not create anyone that is second hand . . .

Maybe you're not a president or a king
But this doesn't mean that you're nothing
And if you are not rich with silver or gold
Don't ever let this make you feel undersold . . .

For these things will not last, they'll fade
Especially the things that are man-made
And the somebody, my friend that you are
Will continue to shine as bright as a star . . .

You are no better or worst than anyone
We're all created equal under the sun
Yes, you are somebody and don't forget it
If you feel otherwise you're sure to regret it. . . . .

## THE WELFARE BLUES

If with the virtue of patience you feel you're well armed
Test it my friend at the Welfare and you'll be most alarmed
For mixed up confusion is the order of the day
Apply for aid in January and hope to get it in May
Their left hand doesn't seem to know it has a right
A most degrading situation will soon be your plight
They act as if the money will be taken from their pay
"Come back tomorrow" is all they ever seem to say
So if need causes you to apply as I have had to do
You'll need the patience of "Job", though they'll try that too . . .

SANDIE WOOD    "Sandie Wood was born in Harlem, New York. He
moved to Roosevelt Treatment Center in Hempstead, L.I. for hospitali-
zation, where he wrote these poems."


# DWIGHT E. REDDICK

## LOST AT SEA

The -
      storm -
   has -
passed -
now. -
The sea;
      not so -
            turbulent.
         Though -
      still -
   not -

calm.
    The -
        wind;
    has -
died.
Though -
            not -
            to -
    light -
breezes.
    The -
            rain -
    has -
ceased.
Though
    dark, -
        heavy, -
            clouds -
        still -
        block -
            the -
        sunlight.
I bob -
        up
and down
in the
swells.
Like a corked -
        bottle -
                tossed to the sea -
        by some marooned, -
    long forgotten, -
seaman.

**44**

My life jacket;
    all that keeps -
        me afloat.
        Above the surface -
      of this seemingly -
    endless sea -
  of -
insanity.
    For fatigue -
would surely -
    pull me -
  down.
Into -
oblivion.
  The peak -
  of a swell -
      and I search -
        the horizon -
          for any -
        sign of -
      land -
      or -
    ship.
    But,
      only -
        the sea.
      Nothing -
    there.
      Only -
    Waves -
      and -
        never -
      ending -

clouds.
I try -
not to -
swim.
Just close -
my eyes -
and float.
Let the -
waves -
take me -
Where -
they -
will.
Sometimes -
I think -
I hear -
the sound -
of waves -
breaking -
upon -
a shore, -
not too
distant.
But,
it -
passes.
Leaving -
only -
the sea. -
The clouds.
Light rain -
and stronger -
winds -

now -
and -
then.
The -
rain -
stops.
The -
wind -
dies.
The sea.
Only the sea.
The clouds.
No land.
No ship.
How long -
has it -
been -
now?
Forever ?
And still -
forever -
to -
go?
Forever.
Lost
at
sea. ————

1989


DWIGHT E. REDDICK   "I am a native Nebraskan (Lincolnite) and
have spent over one half of my almost forty-three years in and out of
both correctional and mental institutions. Now that I have learned to

utilize my emotions in constructive ways, such as writing, the future looks much more promising."


## KAROSELLE WASHINGTON

THE KILLING FLOORS

I really was dismayed at the way the so-called professional people were treating the people who were unfortunate enough to be in this situation. But some people didn't mind being there. Just by what they said and did, happy to sit and watch tv all morning and till into the evening. Happy to eat and consume something I consider unacceptable to eat and look like garbage. We had no one to talk too or to advise us. The few of us who felt we needed encouraging input the staff merely try to treat some of us like dogs patting us on our heads & expecting that to be enough and when we rebelled we weren't cooperating and the drug was either change or the dosage increase. But as I said there were very few who resented being there.

There was only one shower, and only one person could use it at a time, and two bathtubs which took longer to use and most people would shower. They did not have wash cloths, we had to use state underware to wash with. A harsh soap was used, and one can of deodorant for everyone to use. What they called medication would already have been passed out before showering. Sometimes they had Kool Aid, and some of them were stingy and mean if you asked for more. They would sit in the office at night, and would have their dinner. They would cook or send out. Most of the time, they sent out for food. I don't remember any of the night workers giving out anything except one lady who gave away a package of French Fries. She also did my hair and did a good job.

It seemed like everytime I went into the bathroom there was a lethal mess. The women used the toilets and refused or didn't bother to flush them. Sticking toilet paper, clothes and state dresses in the commodes. Some would drag around coffee and spill coffee grinds all over the basins. Cups with coffee in them sat on the basins in spite of the fact, the cleaning women came in everyday to clean. The women still messed up everything, dropping Cigarette Butts on the floor and in cups. It was one big stinking mess all the time. The so called doctors didn't care. All they would say was, are you taking your medicine. I couldn't see why they weren't trying to help us, since it was so obvious we needed help. Everyone needs help now and then. They did not help us and we spent most of the day doing nothing.

In so much all we did the so call patients was to waste our time the shower room was the pitts and just as dangerous as the one over in White Bldg. you could sleep or rest on just the weekends. In Sullivan Bldg. it was impossible you could try to sleep on weekends but with the radio going & people waking you up for cigaretts (I don't smoke) going through your drawers looking for clothes to steal people talking and laughing it was impossible to go back to sleep. In Sullivan Bldg. the people downstairs in lock up felt that it was their right to be able to come upstairs and ask stupid questions. What I didn't understand why nurses didn't insist they stay downstairs mostly in Sullivan Bldg. all you did was to run over to the eating hall to eat. You didn't have all the confusion mostly cause the people who smoke were in one room and the people who didn't sat in the tv room so everybody wasn't all thrown together and people couldn't pick fights weren't together.

In Sullivan Bldg. mornings were always rough considering the older women like to get up before it was time to get up and talk and make coffee and sit on the front row where I was on an empty bed and talk about who knows what. And to top that off there was this one nurse who like to get things going by blaring and playing music loud, singing & dancing & the older women stand behind the glass window and she had big hips and say that's right miss, so & so shake it shake those hips shake it but don't break it all the while people trying to get ready & get up but how could you with all that noise going on and distractions plus they would be always hounding you about making the bed up right. I thought the early morning rackett was inappropriate. Then you were suppose to sit all day in a chair.

Mostly the attitude from the Doctors & social workers & some of the nurses were insolent. Of course you had what they called an hearing but they didn't really want to hear you Judge and I guess a lawyer who never said anything on your behalf it was without a doubt a travesty. Mostly I would just try to fade out on a sofa or curl up in a chair so at six every morning if you reffuse to get out of bed they would say they were going to write you up in the morning the shower rooms were never open. Then the day nurses when come in around seven in the morning people would lay down because they were so tired having just gotten up. So people had to sit up & they didn't have enough furniture then everybody would line up & wait for the first meal, then back to the dayroom people fastly got bored so they would try to lay down again So people even try to watch early morning 6 o'clock TV which got on my nerves.

After awhile they returned they return me. But before I went back there was a group out of Baltimore called paper chase I thought they were preety good I sat in a chair out on the grass I was in a good mood. That was before I got back. The same people were there and some new ones also. I walked back into what they called the dayroom they still did't have a tv but to be honest I really did't care. Someone had a radio the music help to take some of the sting out of being in there pretty soon it was time for lunch. If the food had change I had't notice but nothing had really change there was still those tile marble like walls all those steel mesh windows that surrounded you like they were trying to annoy you and they did . . . One day believe it or not someone bought in a television believe or not everybody gather around it. I guess what it really was it had a sobering affect on everybody people watch the soap opras and talk shows. One girl in her twenties would dominate so fights kept breaking out . . . I did't mind so much sense she like watching the news and so did I there was this woman who wanted to look at rerun situation comedies all the time there was an argument about tv going off for an hour an playing the radio for an hour. It was just one big mess for most of the day I guess what really save us was all those cokes and pepsi and sodas we would send out for by those who went to the store on hour pink cards and they had to be back within an hour . . . the days were a total waste and so were the ones which follow we did't do anything with the time but waste it . . . I couldnt see how other humanbeings could treat other humanbeings like this . . . There attiude was this its not me so I dont give a damn . . . The doctors mainly had this attiude and some of the so called nurses you couldnt convince them why in the hell you had to be there cause you had other places to go something could be arrange with a realtive or grandparents I knew I could had stay with mine since I really stay with her and were just visting at home till I stay a little too long and my father said I was depress and call an ambulance and the police why I really dont know I was minding my own business but to be honest when it came to me could care less abut the way I really felt and that concern everything he would always bother my things my mail and left my sister and brothers junk alone I believe—

KAROSELLE WASHINGTON "I'm 34 about 145-150 lbs I'm light skinned and I'm black. I work part time in a senior citizen day center. I believe in Christ and God. I'm very religious and I believe you should keep yourself for marriage."

EDITOR'S NOTE: What follows are exact transcriptions of selections from giant notebooks in "The Living Museum" at Creedmoor Psychiatric Center, Queens, New York. Under the creative direction of this unusual gallery's "curator," Bolek Greczynski, patients are encouraged to give free written, sculpted or painted expression to their thoughts. From the Creedmoor diary:

## SAMUELA J. BLANK

SEQUELS TO LOLITA

Lolita returns
Son of Lolita
Lolita goes to Oz
Lolita and money
Lolita and men
Lolita and nuclear power
Lolita goes "Back to the Future."
Lolita in steel pyjamas
Lolita almost gets burned at the stake.

Lolita meets the Queen of England.
Lolita "Marries a Millionaire."
Lolita gets divorced.
Lolita on the couch.
Lolita goes solo.
Lolita burns her bra.
Lolita meets Evita!
Lolita meets Beatles.
Lolita pans her own book.
Lolita sings "Don't Stand So Close to Me."*
Lolita joins the C.I.A.
Lolita finds D.N.A.
Lolita joins the Ecumenical Council
Lolitaworld

*This song mentions "That book by Nabokov."

| GOOD SCHIZOPHRENIC | BAD SCHIZOPHRENIC |
|---|---|
| Pays in advance | Doesn't pay his (her) bills |
| Keeps appointments and is never tardy | Misses appointments and is often late |
| Responds to treatment | Is surly |
| Takes medication regularly | Is slipshod about taking his (her) medicine or never takes it. |
| Dresses in good taste | Contradicts the doctor's opinions, diagnoses, etc. |
| Is attractive and preferably is white with blue eyes and blonde hair. | Is overweight and unattractive in other ways. |
| | Sexually harasses or otherwise abuses the M.D. |

## CREEDMOORBLANCA

Scene: Bolek's Place, an art studio in Creedmoorblanca.

Me: "Play it Sam: Play as Time Goes By."
Bolek: "In this crazy world of ours, it doesn't matter a hill of beans what happens to two little people such as us."
Me: "But you must remember this: a kiss is still a kiss a sigh is still a sigh."
Bolek: "The fundamental things apply as time goes by."
          "Play it Sam. You played it for her now you can play it for me."
The End?

## FAUST

I sold my soul for love.
This was no bargain.
I got one husband who died
within ten years.
This isn't going to work
Now I'm in and out of
Creedmoor, and I wish I
could sell my sould to stay out of here.
First I have to buy it back.
I should have sold it for money.

SAMUELA BLANK   "My name is Samuela Joy Blank. I am in my forties. When I was in my twenties I went to City College and worked as a model. Before this sounds like an ad for the 'personal' columns in *New York* magazine, I would like to say that I am the widow of a social worker and I now live in an adult home. My favorite author is George Orwell."

## MY DREAM

My little country cottage with a swimming pool. A flowered grassy lawn, a worthwhile life from daw 'till dawn. A mate, one child or two, maybe a little pet. An old vision—still worth something yet—a family car for my luxury house.

Comfortably furnished, carpeted + draped. A fireplace in the den to warm us in the frost. And smoke from the chimney so we don't get lost.

---

I am a Fraud!
I am not this person. I have no name!
Property: I have none
Family: I have none
Friends: Sometimes on "fair days"
Talents: Dreaming. Talent for getting in trouble for getting angry even though it's the proper reaction to this place!

I have talent to pretend + dream end on end—I am a space baby that may live 4 ever, my brain seems to be preserved but it is still small, still in all, I like the very young, the very new. New and young life! Only with the new do I feel the breezes blow, only with the very young can I truly enjoy life!

JO ANN KALISH   "I've had my ups and downs, struggling to overcome my mental illness, trying to remain cheerful while enjoying reading, poetry, art and music."

# RANDY MAIONE

It's time to eat
I feasted last night
But tomorrow I'll go
on a food binge
Times lost and I seem
to watch the clock
for noon time
Now I got so fat

RANDY MAIONE   "is a 31 year old single, Catholic high school graduate. Born on 1/24/59 in Korea and brought to U.S.A. at age 5. She was adopted by a Maione family at the age of 8. There is no information about her early developmental history prior to her adoption . . . Randy became mentally ill at the age of 17 when she began college. Subsequently, she was almost continuously hospitalized since 1981 to the present times." (Courtesy Creedmoor Psychiatric Center)

# TIMOTHY T. TONRY

Every time it rains
it remembers me of the
          Pain
Every sunny day I wish
          would go away
Then came yesterday
I spent the day and
          night awake
Thinking and feeling
          Great

Forgiven the unforgiving
Remembering the
        unremember
Stars + Stripes
        Forever

1984

TIMOTHY T. TONRY   "Born in Brooklyn, Bay Ridge. Parochial
schools . . . Hope to attend St. John's University in September. Study
literature and publishing. Went to Viet Nam in the Army. Disability
discharge in 1968. Since I was 20 I have been hospitalized. I am now 42
years old and in remission. . . . I believe in the truth, good education,
and God." (Courtesy Creedmoor Psychiatric Center)

## BLANCHE TEMPLETONNAGE

LAMENT

A doctor a day keeps the apple away
The steaks and the chops were not here to stay
My posterior's spreading
My hair's turning grey
The patience of Job is
   exhausted today

1985

It occurs to me now that I'm going to jail.
I've inserted my thumb in a toy beagle's tail.

The canine belongs to a lady named Gail
If wardens' and guards' tender mercies should fail,
  I won't be paroled on the court's posted bail

1985


BLANCHE TEMPLETONNAGE    "I should like to leave this labyrin-
thine world of mental-ill health which relies upon the zoological
classifications of the 'Reader's Indigestion' and to realize my dream of
becoming wealthy in the recognition of my incomparable intellect
and, in spite of the persecutors of my livelyhood and well being. I
represent myself only as BLANCHE TEMPLETONNAGE."



# JANE PRETTO

Today I remembered the day
                isn't important.
Nor the year
It's how I look, feel and what
                I fear
If it's in Gregg or Pittman
                Hindu or Greek
Whatever have you—
When I don't know the day
I feel weak.

| January  | 1234567890 | etc. | 1900's |
| February | 1234567890 | etc. | "      |
| March    | 1234567890 | etc. | "      |
| April    | 1234567890 | etc. | "      |
| May      | 1234567890 | etc. | "      |
| June     | 1234567890 | etc. | "      |

| July       | 1234567890 | etc. | " |
| August     | 1234567890 | etc. | " |
| September  | 1234567890 | etc. | " |
| October    | 1234567890 | etc. | " |
| November   | 1234567890 | etc. | " |
| December   | 1234567890 | etc. | " |

1985

---

## UNTITLED

Fortnight til noontide I await your call.
Fort'nite until noontide aye await your caul.
Fort night til noontide I await you're caul.
Fort'knight til noontide aye await you're caul.
Fort night 'til noontide I await you're call.
Fort Knight. Till noontide! Aye. A-wait! You're caul.
"Fortknight till noontide," "Aye!" A, wait your call.
Fort/night til noontide I aweight your call.
Fort'Knight till noon tied. Aye, aweight yore call.

1985

---

Today I don't feel so good
If I thought really that tomorrow
could be better, I'd be happy:
But, I doubt it. I doubt
tomorrow will be better.
I doubt it very much.
I worry now. I worry because they locked me away and hurt
me and I'm afraid of being hurt again. It's been 14 years away
from home in hospitals. And every night that I slept made every
day another day of sickness. And I want privacy so much, and

**59**

then some clock keeps saying, I can't be left alone. Oh, I hope it's just the day. I hope I'm not this tired and sleepy for the rest of my life. If I am then I'm better off dead. And then I'll see. And then maybe I'll find someone to kill me. I'll wait and see. My dad must my sleepy too. So must Chuck. Chuck, my husband, was sick. I hope he's okay now. I hope it was just because I was sick. I hope me + dad + mom + Chuck are all better soon.

What if no one ever comes here to get me? What if I'm locked away in these rooms with 100's of people (strangers) for the rest of my life. Then I'll try and find someone to kill me. If you know, maybe you can take me by surprise.

JANE PRETTO    "The most important part of me isn't clear for me to see I love painting and writing and my gosh! isn't it always a surprise."

## RICHARD LAX

UTOPIAN SPACE BIBLE—<u>GOD</u>
(THE ETERNAL QUEST)

Introductory Prayer—

"See God, King of Creation, Lord of Life your slave-rigger Atom, a star going Nova (heart attack) burning out in search of himself. . . ."

Alternate Opening—

In the beginning of the Space Age, God's slave-rigger Atom, a star going Nova (heart attack) burning out in search of himself . . .

UTOPIAN SPACE BIBLE
(for the greater glory of God and Spain)

In the age of Space-time beginning in 1957 (A.A.—after Atom, a new age, the Space age) God's slave rigger Atom on planet Hellose conquered a mountain named Duston (Mt. Fear) at the remotest ends of the Universes full of aliens (unto themselves) and was trying to make planet Hellose (Earth) into planet Godose (a Utopian God planet) with the help of Duster— Rhiannon (Duston), and Serianna (Queen of planet Hellose).

I sing the fate, excruciating agonies, tortures, trials, tribulations and hells of young Atom and Messiah of planet Godose.

"Across the vastnesses of Space-time Atom journeyed in search of the heart and mind of God to commingle with. . . .

"Atom sought the Kingly King of Creation thru Universalism, the Upconscious Mind and Uprealism. . . .

"The Suferians (first space time Civilization) had force marched young Atom to walk thru and around their entire planet in an ordeal or test by fire radiation. . . . Yes, the Suferians had made young Atom march the 25,000 miles across the face of the earth and all the thousands of miles around the planet which took him half a lifetime figured in current life spans of approximately 70 years.

"The Suferian Corporation (Sufer Corp. for short because they had made such a serious business of Life due to their self-denying & flagellating Stoic philosophy) had chosen young Atom as their disciple & chief Messiah in order to bring about the required blast-off from their Earthly cradle of Hell known as planet Hellose.

"Young Atom was born at the "crossroads of the universes" (Main Street, Flushing, Queens) and was presently in a severe quandary—what to do about the many people who'd given their very lives for him, thinking him better than a modern-day Jesus and seeing him as the supreme Suferian in his ability to tolerate pain, agony and torture. Each strategic person in his life had died for a definite purpose so that he might singlehandedly save planet Hellose from nuclear destruction. Atom was a little guilt stricken about it all from the sheer awesomeness of knowledge that God had chosen him as planet Hellose's Savior with all those dead friends of young Atom's behind him.

RICHARD LAX   "This is a 44 year old white, Jewish male who is the oldest of 3 siblings, having 2 younger sisters . . . Mr. Lax completed 2½ years of college and had an extensive work history. His mental illness and subsequent psychiatric hospitalizations date back to March 1975 when he was 28 years of age." (Courtesy Creedmoor Psychiatric Center)

## ANONYMOUS

As the inner world
   reveals the outer
goosesteps resound the
   darkness

I wish breathtaking were
   my leave
I wish departure were
   my clue
I die in she-devil:
   she devily arms

EDITOR'S NOTE: This anonymous poem was painted on a door at the Living Museum. This poem ends the selection from Creedmoor.

I was eighteen years old when they had the gall to send me to a place for being "mixed-up;" the Institute. They sent me to one of those expensive ones that had a swimming pool and a golf course, but I never saw the light of the day. I was quite angry at them for this, but what could I do? I was under age, and times were primitive.

## REMINISCENCES

1. This hospital is a nightmare of blazing white lights, and out of this comes this black death-doctor to tell me today my Dad was coming to see me. And, damnit, he's supposed to have left for the Congo, and I don't want to see him, but hell, they're all a bunch of deceitful bastards. This damned therapy, and then the shocks rip you apart. I'm really OK. They put these pads on your temples, but I'm really OK and unchanged. I will always remain the high-geared and erratic soul with just another layer of pain and confusion added to my freckled skin. There were long corridors, locked doors, prim white nurses with uncommitted faces and keys jangling at their waists. Sometimes I'd get really doped up and it'd be like I was floating with this sedation in a lovely heaven of roulette wheels, spinning reds and blacks that look like me in the night, and drive-in movies and food and wine, and beautiful voices. Still, I am resentful of life, perhaps because my mother called me a walrus when I cried, but I am curable because I have faith in a few people. If I didn't have faith in you, I would throw a tomato at daddy-o and then run and hide for the rest of time, and let them come and find me in death's dream kingdom. I'm too scared to face the iron man, but when I come out of hiding, I will go native and wave tomatoes at him. The time has come to sleep and forget and be feelless, but

as always, the weather is different from when I was a child, and there are so few men and women left. Well, it went like this. They were yellow, red, royal blue, blue and red, all the colors and sizes you could imagine. Hooked? Sure. They gave me God and hell all wrapped up together and never did I really know where I was at. But I once had a dealer and a bit of money and the r would arrive in the mail right on their monthly schedule. But Jesus, it was safe. I mean no o.d.s, no kicking the habit cold turkey, no cell block scenes or fingers up my ass. Then came this nut-hut scene which was different, where more boring colors like brown or muddy green are prescribed. I mean, of course, things like the phenothizines which make your belly blow, your eyes rivet to the sky, your hands palsied and your brain worthless. There was Dr. Adam Flynn, a notorious neurologist, whose gospel was thorazine and whose understanding of the human soul would have made a roach look promising.

"It's not working as well anymore. It's like I'm getting immune to it."

"What about the other stuff you take?"

"You mean the thorazine and. . ."

"Yes. It seems to me that that could make your head that way."

"But that's a whole different thing. I mean, I have to take that stuff every day and my head is sometimes OK even when I'm taking it so that's not consistent—"

"Yet you've told me that you have a thorazine belly—you think that's really the thorazine?"

"Yes, and I'll tell you why. I figure that after being on those heavy drugs for as long as I have, it's got to have some effect on my metabolism. It's like this—you know how they put ID + into neutral fields, just pump it in from the outside, impose it on the fields, and what this does is completely destroy the internal ecological balance. . ."

"I see. So you figure that's the way with the thorazine. But if you feel that way, why do you take it?"

"That's two things going the opposite way. I mean, I take it because I've been in a world for awhile where you're constantly told that the medicine is the key to keeping you on the level. After hearing that for five-six years, I figure I've got to take it because if I suddenly stop like because I don't believe in it, I'll fall apart."

"But you don't believe it does any good?"

"No. Hell, I take it no matter what's going on inside me and if things are good they stay the same. If they're bad, they stay the same—no difference in feeling."

"But you're getting it all confused—"

"No. That's what I mean about the two things going the opposite ways—knowing one way that makes no difference except like maybe giving me a belly because it's an unnatural chemical getting messed with my natural (metabolic) chemicals, and then the other way feeling it's like some power that maybe holds me together without my really feeling, knowing it—"

"But really, you're saying you're psychologically dependent on it."

"That's it—I am and it's a rough thing. If I miss sometimes like if I don't have a dose on me when I'm out, I get nervous, really uptight."

"Do you think you'll ever be off it?"

"Oh, yes—now I'm down to twice, and someday soon it'll be once, and then off."

"I see. It has to be slow."

"Sure. It's too much to cut it quick."

But there are beautiful colors left, all reds and blacks and the gold you get in the damn sun, and beauty too, and hell, I'll be OK sometime. Last night I shot thirty light bulbs with a beebee gun in the dining room just for kicks, and man what a panic was breaking out there. Sometimes the sun is good for people. Not me. I turn red like a crimson crack in a black cloud zigzagging in a midst of blood and the sun turns dark and shows through the bottom.

2. I've got scurvy, a salt deficiency, and a scar on my right arm. Good for laughs. Really, I've got rigor mortis. Sweet dreams my heavenly playmates, and remember even French jazz isn't really soothing, only gold crosses that hang over one's sleeping head and golden people floating around you in a dreamy haze. When awake I feel like I am a derailed freight train that forgot it was supposed to run on tracks. Now, as always, the fatigue disease is hitting me, and the time has come to cease and desist. Sweet, sweet dreams to all and drink so much like oily godly creatures should and have a bottle of red wine and remember me. My head was full of rainbows, greedy for ecstasy, but as all such people, I walked a high wire and often wondered what the results would be if all my feverish energy became channeled. Eventually that space and time and boundaries of dimensions disappear and there is no more me, no more chunky body, no needs, no pain, only that whirling high. So high I am God freed from the cross.

3. Lately I have been feeling like the worst part of a bad novel, and they put the wires to my head every week now. But God cannot commit suicide: he is eternal by definition, poor trapped bastard. Time got left somewhere in the sky many years ago leaving everyone on the brink of violence while I am on the brink of emptiness, as one outsider might say to another. People are beginning to close in to crush me like I want to crush them. I lost contact with my mind months ago, so I need to come home and put myself back on the road to goodness and God, and all the luscious white storks. I am alone in my little white room playing solitaire and listening to Mexican songs and wondering whatever happened to time that there's none left. But you see,

I'm learning to cut out paper dolls. Children don't really know how, and I'm really happy because I can really do it. Soon, too, all can know the real meaning of a paper doll. Too much too soon, and all of it revolving around paper dolls and storks and everything is red and black on the cards on the table, my black soul, and my red blood, black books with black bindings and red hands with red scars and too much intensity. You know, when I look parallel with a candle, I am God. For each man kills the thing he loves. Stolen F.B.I. bicycle, incredible speed down a beautifully long hill, water on each side, black-boy and it's thought to be incarcerated filth, steal a philodendrum leaf, it's all relative. A little powder and things get better, watermelon and asparagus equals a kidney flush. At least the doors are varnished, not yellow today. Can't get God, water doesn't leave stains, have to die because I can't see the bridge of my nose? But why not if you can only see it cross-eyed? N.B.: no letters to my dead ancestors tonight, have to join them and beat the live ones to the game, won't get accredited if you die. My hands are too small and they're yellow like everything else, tired, I guess, of being too small. Can't get clean, stripped of rights and dignity by one's own volition. They say you're in a sanitarium and it's a sea of waste, human. Muddled vision or simply humanitarianism? Essentially atavistic. Better to cut the umbilical cord before it's too late and then chalk it up to poor genes. Inbreeding? Deficient enzymes? It's all insignificant, but if you don't pretend it's significant you're through, no one cares, but who cares if anyone cares? You kick the system or you don't and if you don't, you're a failure. Admit it and eradicate self-pity. Purple flowers from the swamp. No person, no death.

4. Full of locks and keys and tunnels. There is so much pain that sometimes I am suffocated by the thought that there's no end, maybe it's all too complicated to penetrate the rottenness in the human heart and soul. And yet there could be so many golden

apples. It could be off. Olympus with Gods and Angels and Queens and golds. Green is the color of hope and you, my children, are gold.

No person, no death: "But I being poor have only my dreams." Essence of a winter's lust. The low relevancy twist isn't enough, scars re-opened and no release. True, God is a farce, but maybe that's the only way to make it, purple sunset on the Potamic and then rain. I'm in yellow, you're in black. The brain is a mass of synthetic jelly and hooked on platitudes. Maybe the astronauts did say they would fly over my house, or maybe it's disintegration (without dignity). "Only God can love you for yourself alone, my dear, and not your yellow hair." Guilt creates the Gods. It's difficult to incarcerate a 300-lb. sodden mass, but get it stripped down, and it comes easy. One can feel the brain cells disintegrating, a few at a time, fed on honeydew too often. Mental note: Dear mother, I'm sorry I haven't been able to visit your grave too often in the past few weeks, but you know how things are: wonder, eat fudgies and sublimate your questionable desires. But I'm in yellow and my gods, I can't reach them enough even to be subjugated. What's a note? My life and it's ripped up, the illusions are all that remain. Take enough poison by small doses, your body becomes immune and you have them caught. Last Will and Testament: a carton of Cokes, meaningless words and dead gods. It's all an equation that adds up to No Return. The tomato, or maybe perhaps the watermelon, explodes. Result? Scattered seeds and a little excess juice.

## NOTES

Mama Cass, heart turned to fat. Hereford cows OK, but it's got to be French vanilla. Red clay earth. Unpainted furniture, a little polyurethane. The big C sets in—afraid? Me? No! Heinz 57 sauce—according to the radio. Left his legs in Vietnam, grated

Parmesan and Romano cheese—out the hole on top. Sorry, but God hasn't called yet, though he's due around 11 p.m. Can't say I'm proud of all the things I've done, nip away at the gin plus vodka 'til it's all gone and then you really feel welcome at. (Well, hell, she shouldn't serve out noodles for dinner when she knows I'm dieting. Mother-in-law? No, rather have the father-in-law pass on my soul. Please tell me where the answer lies. Does it lie in his eyes?—ain't gonna be no auxiliary cop—Sorry, but my life's on wheels as it is. Maybe I'm being foolish and I haven't heard you mention anybody's name at all. Hit a candle parallel and you got God—greens not gold, my children. Sleep well, remember no time for honky-tonk angels tonight, just the eternal lover's question.

## NOTES

Clothiers and Furnishers. Previous seasons (but who could really tell the difference?): suits, sportcoats, topcoats, tweeds, hats, reduced 20%. Just remember current season's merchandise is available but *not* reduced. So you want a hair transplant! I'm having daydreams about night-things in the middle of the afternoon. Reds and blacks, they mold together and form what? Bliss or a roulette wheel? All you really need to do is buy some Heinz 57 sauce, but you have to remember that it's not 10 oz. but 284 gr. Dying? Yes, I guess I need space. I'm scared and angry as hell. Who took the nunnery from me? A smashed world and no more deviled eggs. Can't eat them now, but I guess that's the breaks of the game. Kumquats? No, I wouldn't return to California for them, but maybe an abalone shell would make the trip worth it.

MARY RAND   Mary grew up in Southern California, attending the Katherine Branson School in Marin County. She went on to Vassar

College, and lived most of her adult life in New York City. She was a junior tennis champion, and eventually received a Masters of Education at Teacher's College, although it was her ambition to devote herself to writing and painting. Hospitalized for long periods, Mary killed herself in December, 1985 after a long and heroic struggle against a ravaging psychiatric disorder. (Courtesy Peter Rand)

## MARY MACLANE

Butte, Montana, January 13, 1901

I of womankind and of nineteen years, will now begin to set down as full and frank a Portrayal as I am able of myself, Mary MacLane, for whom the world contains not a parallel.

I am convinced of this, for I am odd.

I am distinctly original innately and in development.

I have in me a quite unusual intensity of life.

I can feel.

I have a marvelous capacity for misery and for happiness.

I am broad-minded.

I am a genius.

I am a philosopher of my own good peripatetic school.

I care neither for right nor for wrong—my conscience is nil.

My brain is a conglomeration of aggressive versatility.

I have reached a truly wonderful state of miserable morbid unhappiness.

I know myself, oh, very well.

I have attained an egotism that is rare indeed.

I have gone into the deep shadows.

All this constitutes oddity. I find therefore, that I am quite, quite odd.

I have hunted for even the suggestion of a parallel among the several hundred persons that I call acquaintances. But in vain. There are people and people of varying depths and intricacies of character, but there is none to compare with me. The young ones of my own age—if I chance to give them but a glimpse of the real workings of my mind—can only stare at me in dazed stupidity uncomprehending; and the old ones of forty and fifty—for forty and fifty are always old to nineteen—can but either stare also in stupidity, or else, their own narrowness asserting itself, smile their little devilish smile of superiority which they reserve indiscriminately for all foolish young things. The utter idiocy of forty and fifty at times!

These, to be sure, are extreme instances. There are among my young acquaintances some who do not stare in stupidity, and yes, even at forty and fifty there are some who understand some phases of my complicated character, though none to comprehend it in its entirety.

But, as I said, even the suggestion of a parallel is not to be found among them.

Along some lines I have gotten to the edge of the world. A step more and I fall off. I do not take the step. I stand on the edge, and I suffer.

Nothing, oh, nothing on the earth can suffer like a woman young and all alone!

—Before proceeding farther with the Portraying of Mary Mac-Lane, I will write out some of her uninteresting history.

I was born in 1881 at Winnepeg, in Canada. Whether Winnepeg will yet live to be proud of this fact is a matter for some conjecture and anxiety on my part. When I was four years old I was taken with my family to a little town in western Minnesota, where I lived a more or less vapid and lonely life until I was ten. We came then to Montana.

Whereat the aforesaid life was continued.

My father died when I was eight.

Apart from feeding and clothing me comfortably and sending me to school—which is no more than was due me—and transmitting to me the MacLane blood and character, I can not see that he ever gave me a single thought.

Certainly he did not love me, for he was quite incapable of loving any one but himself. And since nothing is of any moment in this world without the love of human beings for each other, it is a matter of supreme indifference to me whether my father, Jim MacLane of selfish memory, lived or died.

He is nothing to me.

There are with me still a mother, a sister, and two brothers.

They also are nothing to me.

They do not understand me any more than if I were some strange live curiosity, as which I dare say they regard me. . . .

There is absolutely no sympathy between my immediate family and me. There can never be. My mother, having been with me during the whole of my nineteen years, has an utterly distorted idea of my nature and its desires, if indeed she has any idea of it.

When I think of the exquisite love and sympathy which might be between a mother and daughter, I feel myself defrauded of a beautiful thing rightfully mine, in a world where for me such things are pitiably few.

It will always be so.

My sister and brothers are not interested in me and my analyses and philosophy, and my wants. Their own are strictly practical and material. The love and sympathy between human beings is to them, it seems, a thing only for people in books.

In short, they are Lowland Scotch, and I am a MacLane.

And so, as I've said, I carried my uninteresting existence into Montana. The existence became less uninteresting, however, as my versatile mind began to develop and grow and know the glittering things that are. But I realized as the years were passing that my own life was at best a vapid, negative thing.

A thousand treasures that I wanted were lacking.

I graduated from the high school with these things: very good Latin; good French and Greek; indifferent geometry and other mathematics; a broad conception of history and literature; peripatetic philosophy that I acquired without any aid from the high school; genius of a kind, that has always been with me; an empty heart that has taken on a certain wooden quality; an excellent strong young woman's-body; a pitiably starved soul.

With this equipment I have gone my way through the last two years. But my life, though unsatisfying and warped, is no longer insipid. It is fraught with a poignant misery—the misery of nothingness.

I have no particular thing to occupy me. I write every day. Writing is a necessity—like eating. I do a little housework, and on the whole I am rather fond of it—some parts of it. I dislike dusting chairs, but I have no aversion to scrubbing floors. Indeed, I have gained much of my strength and gracefulness of body from scrubbing the kitchen floor—to say nothing of some fine points of philosophy. It brings a certain energy to one's body and to one's brain.

But mostly I take walks far away in the open country. Butte and its immediate vicinity present as ugly an outlook as one could wish to see. It's so ugly indeed that it is near the perfection of ugliness. And anything perfect, or nearly so, is not to be despised. I have reached some astonishing subtleties of conception as I have walked for miles over the sand and barrenness among the little hills and gulches. Their utter desolateness is an inspiration to the long, long thoughts and to the nameless wanting. Every day I walk over the sand and barrenness.

And so, then, my daily life seems an ordinary life enough, and possibly, to an ordinary person, a comfortable life.

That's as may be.

To me it is an empty, damned weariness.

I rise in the morning; eat three meals; and walk; and work a little, read a little, write; see some uninteresting people; go to bed.

Next day, I rise in the morning; eat three meals; and walk; and work a little, read a little, write; see some uninteresting people; go to bed.

Again I rise in the morning; eat three meals; and walk; and work a little, read a little, write; see some uninteresting people; go to bed.

Truly an exalted, soulful life!

What it does for me, how it affects me, I am now trying to portray.

## January 24

I am charmingly original. I am delightfully refreshing. I am startlingly Bohemian. I am quaintly interesting—the while in my sleeve I may be smiling and smiling—and a villain. I can talk to a roomful of dull people and compel their interest, admiration, and astonishment. I do this sometimes for my own amusement. As I have said, I am a rather plain-featured, insignificant-looking genius, but I have a graceful personality. I have a pretty figure. I am well-set up. And when I choose to talk in my charmingly original fashion, embellishing my conversation with many quaint lies, I have a certain very noticeable way with me, an "air."

It is well, if one has nothing else, to acquire an air. And an air taken in conjunction with my charming originality, my delightfully refreshing candor, is something powerful and striking in its way.

I do not, however, exert myself often in this way; partly because I can sometimes foresee, from the character of the assembled company, that my performance will not have the desired effect—for I am a genius, and genius at close range at times carries itself unconsciously to the point where it becomes so interesting that it is atrocious, and can not be carried farther without having somewhat mildly diastrous results; and then, again, the facial antics of some ten or a dozen persons possessed more or less of the qualities of the genus fool—even they become tiresome after a while.

Always I talk about myself on an occasion of this kind. Indeed, my conversation is on all occasions devoted directly or indirectly to myself.

When I talk on the subject of ethics, I talk of it as it is related to Mary MacLane.

When I give out broad-minded opinions about Ninon de l'Enclos, I demonstrate her relative position to Mary MacLane!

When I discourse liberally on the subject of the married relation, I talk of it only as it will affect Mary MacLane.

An interesting creature, Mary MacLane.

As a matter of fact, it is so with every one, only every one is far from realizing and acknowledging it. And I have not lacked listeners, though these people do not appreciate me. They do not realize that I am a genius.

I am of womankind and of nineteen years. I am able to stand off and gaze critically and dispassionately at myself and my relation to my environment, to the world, to everything the world contains. I am able to judge whether I am good and whether I am bad. I am able, indeed, to tell what I am and where I stand. I can see far, far inward. I am a genius.

Charlotte Bronté did this in some degree, and she was a genius; and also Marie Bashkirtseff, and Olive Schreiner, and George Eliot. They are all geniuses.

And so, then, I am a genius—a genius in my own right.

I am fundamentally, organically egotistic. My vanity and self-conceit have attained truly remarkable development as I've walked and walked in the loneliness of the sand and barrenness. Not the least remarkable part of it is that I know my egotism and vanity thoroughly—thoroughly, and plume myself thereon.

These are the ear-marks of a genius—and of a fool. There is a finely-drawn line between a genius and a fool. Often this line is overstepped and your fool becomes a genius, or your genius becomes a fool.

It is but a tiny step.

There's but a tiny step between the great and the little, the tender and the contemptuous, the sublime and the ridiculous, the aggressive and the humble, the paradise and the perdition.

And so is it between the genius and the fool.

I am a genius.

I am not prepared to say how many times I may overstep the finely-drawn line, or how many times I have already overstepped it. 'Tis a matter of small moment.

I have entered into certain things marvelously deep. I know things, I know that I know them, and I know that I know that I know them, which is a fine psychological point.

It is magnificent of me to have gotten so far, at the age of nineteen, with no training other than that of the sand and barrenness. Magnificent—do you hear?

Very often I take this fact in my hand and squeeze it hard like an orange, to get the sweet, sweet juice from it. I squeeze a great deal of juice from it every day, and every day the juice is renewed, like the vitals of Prometheus. And so I squeeze and squeeze, and drink the juice, and try to be satisfied.

Yes, you may gaze long and curiously at the portrait in the front of this book. It is of one who is a genius of egotism and analysis, a genius who is awaiting the Devil's coming—a genius, with a wondrous liver within.

I shall tell you more about this liver, I think, before I have done.

## January 27

This is not a diary. It is a Portrayal. It is my inner life shown in its nakedness. I am trying my utmost to show everything—to reveal every petty vanity and weakness, every phase of feeling, every desire. It is a remarkably hard thing to do, I find, to probe my soul to its depths, to expose its shades and half-lights.

Not that I am troubled with modesty or shame. Why should one be ashamed of anything?

But there are elements in one's mental equipment so vague, so opaque, so undefined—how is one to grasp them? I have analyzed and analyzed, and I have gotten down to some extremely fine points—yet still there are things upon my own horizon that go beyond me.

There are feelings that rise and rush over me overwhelmingly. I am helpless, crushed, and defeated, before them. It is as if they were written on the walls of my soul-chamber in an unknown language.

My soul goes blindly seeking, seeking, asking. Nothing answers. I cry out after some unknown Thing with all the strength of my being; every nerve and fiber in my young woman's-body and my young woman's-soul reaches and strains in anguished unrest. At times as I hurry over my sand and barrenness all my life's manifold passions culminate in utter rage and woe. Waves of intense, hopeless longing rush over me and envelop me round and round. My heart, my soul, my mind go wandering—wandering; ploughing their way through darkness with never a ray of light; groping with helpless hands; asking, longing, wanting things: pursued by a Demon of Unrest.

I shall go mad—I shall go mad, I say over and over to myself. But no. No one goes mad. The Devil does not propose to release any one from a so beautifully-wrought, artistic damnation. He looks to it that one's senses are kept fully intact, and he fastens to them with steel chains the Demon of Unrest.

It hurts—oh, it tortures me in the days and days! But when the Devil brings me my Happiness I will forgive him all this.

When my Happiness is given me, the Unrest will still be with me, I doubt not, but the Happiness will change the tenor of it, will make it an instrument of joy, will clasp hands with it and mingle itself with it—the while I, with my wooden heart, my woman's-body, my mind, my soul, shall be in transports. I shall be filled with pleasure so deep and pain so intense that my being's minutest nerve will reel and stagger in intoxication, will go drunk with the fullness of Life.

When my Happiness is given me I shall live centuries in the hours. And we shall all grow old rapidly—I and my wooden heart, and my woman's-body, and my mind, and my soul. Sorrow may age one in some degree. But Happiness—the real Happiness—rolls countless years off from one's fingertips in a single moment, and each year leaves its impress.

It is true that life is a tragedy to those who feel. When my Happiness is given me life will be an ineffable, a nameless thing.

It will seethe and roar; it will plunge and whirl; it will leap and shriek in convulsion; it will quiver in delicate fantasy; it will writhe and twist; it will glitter and flash and shine; it will sing gently; it will shout in exquisite excitement; it will vibrate to the roots like a great oak in a storm; it will dance; it will glide; it will gallop; it will rush; it will swell and surge; it will fly; it will soar high—high: it will go down into depths unexplored; it will rage and rave; it will yell in utter joy; it will melt; it will blaze; it will ride triumphant; it will grovel in the dust of entire pleasure; it will sound out like a terrific blare of trumpets; it will chime faintly, faintly like the remote tinkling notes of a harp; it will sob and grieve and weep; it will revel and carouse; it will shrink; it will go in pride; it will lie prone like the dead; it will float bouyantly on air; it will moan, shiver, burst—oh, it will reek with Love and Light!

The words of the English language are futile. There are no words in it, or in any other, to express an idea of that thing which would be my life in its Happiness.

The words I have written describe it, it is true—but confusedly and inadequately.

But words are for everyday use.

When it comes my turn to meet face to face the unspeakable vision of the Happy Life I shall be rendered dumb.

But the rains of my feeling will come in torrents!

February 12

I am in no small degree, I find, a sham—a player to the gallery. Possibly this may be felt as you read these analyses.

While all of these emotions are written in the utmost seriousness and sincerity, and are exactly as I feel them, day after day—so far as I have the power to express what I feel—still I aim to convey through them all the idea that I am lacking in the grand element of Truth—that there is in the warp and woof of my life a thread that is false—false.

I don't know how to say this without the fear of being misunderstood. When I say I am in a way a sham, I have no reference to the truths as I have given them in this Portrayal, but to a very light and subtle thing that runs through them.

Oh, do not think for an instant that this analysis of my emotions is not perfectly sincere and real, and that I have not felt

all of them more than I can put into words. They are my tears—
my life-blood!

But in my life, in my personality, there is an essence of falseness
and insincerity. A thin, fine vapor of fraud hangs always over me
and dampens and injures some things in me that I value.

I have not succeeded thoroughly in analyzing this—it is so
thin, so elusive, so faint—and yet not little. It is a natural thing
enough viewed in the light of my other traits.

I have lived my nineteen years buried in an environment at
utter variance with my natural instincts, where my inner life is
never touched, and my sympathies very rarely, if ever, appealed
to. I never disclose my real desires or the texture of my soul.
Never, that is to say, to any one except my one friend, the
anemone lady.—And so every day of my life I am playing a part;
I am keeping an immense bundle of things hidden under my
cloak. When one has played a part—a false part—all one's life,
for I was a sly, artful little liar even in the days of five and six;
then one is marked. One may never rid oneself of the mantle of
falseness, charlatanry—particularly if one is innately a liar.

A year ago when the friendship of my anemone lady was
given me, and she would sometimes hear sympathetically some
long-silent bit of pain, I felt a snapping of tense-drawn cords, a
breaking away of flood-gates—and a strange, new pain. I felt as if
I must clasp her gentle hand tightly and give way to the pent-up,
surging tears of eighteen years. I had wanted this tender thing
more than anything else all my life, and it was given me suddenly.

I felt a convulsion and a melting, within.

But I could not tell my one friend exactly what I felt. There
was no doubt in my own mind as to my own perfect sincerity of
feeling, but there was with it and around it this vapor of fraud, a
spirit of falseness that rose and confronted me and said, "hypo-
crite," "fool."

It may be that the spirit of falseness is itself a false thing—yet true or false, it is with me always. I have tried, in writing out my emotions, to convey an idea of this sham element while still telling everything faithfully true. Sometimes I think I have succeeded, and at other times I seem to have signally failed. This element of falseness is absolutely the very thinnest, the very finest, the rarest of all the things in my many-sided character.

It is not the most unimportant.

I have seen visions of myself walking in various pathways. I have seen myself trying one pathway and another. And always it is the same: I see before me in the path, darkening the way and filling me with dread and discouragement, a great black shadow—the shadow of my own element of falseness.

I can not rid myself of it.

I am an innate liar.

This is a hard thing to write about. Of all things it is the most liable to be misunderstood. You will probably misunderstand it, for I have not succeeded in giving the right idea of it. I aimed at it and missed it. It eluded me completely. . . .

But this is a complete Portrayal of me—as I await the Devil's coming—and I must tell everything—everything.

When the lead is in the sky and in my life, a vision of Badness looms up on the horizon and looks at me and beckons with a fascinating finger. Then I say to myself, What is the use of this unsullied, struggling soul; this unbesmirched, empty heart; this treasureless, innocent mind; this insipid maid's-body? There are no good things for them. But here, to be sure, are fascinating, glittering bad things—the goods that the gods provide, the compensation of the Devil.

Comes Death, some day, I said—but to die, in the sight of glittering bad things—and I only nineteen! These glittering things appear fair.

There is really nothing evil in the world. Some things appear distorted and unnatural because they have been badly done. Had they been perfect in conception and execution they would strike one only with admiration at their fine, iridescent lights. You remember Don Juan and Haidee. That, to be sure, was not evil in any event—they loved each other. But if they had had only a passing, if intense, fancy for one another, who would call it evil? Who would call it anything but wonderful, charming, enchanting? The Devil's bad things—like the Devil's good things—may gleam and glisten, oh, how they may gleam and glisten! I have seen them do so, not only in a poem of Byron's, but in the life that is.

Always when the lead is in the sky I would like to cultivate thoroughly this branch of the vineyard. Now doesn't it make you shiver to think of this dear little Mary MacLane wandering unloved through dark by-ways and deadly labyrinths? It makes me shiver. But it needn't. If I am to wander unloved, why not as well wander there as through Nothingness?

I fancy it must be wonderfully easy to become used to the many-sided Badness. I have lived my nineteen years in the midst of Nothingness, and I have not yet become used to it. It has sharp knives in it, has Nothingness. Badness may have some sharp knives also—but there are other things. Yes, there are other things.

Kind Devil, if you are not to fetch me Happiness, then slip off from your great steel key-ring a bright little key to the door of the glittering, gleaming bad things, and give it me, and show me the way, and wish me joy.

I would like to live about seven years of judicious Badness, and then Death, if you will. Nineteen years of damnable Nothingness, seven years of judicious Badness—and then Death. A noble ambition! But might it not be worse? If not that, then nineteen years of damnable Nothingness, and then

Death. No; when the lead is in the sky that does not appeal to me. My versatile mind turns to the seven years of judicious Badness.

There is nothing in the world without its element of Badness. It is in literature; it is in every art—in pictures, sculpture, even in music. There are certain fine, deep, minute passages in Beethoven and in Chopin that tell of things wonderfully, sublimely bad. Chopin one can not understand. Is there any one in the world who can understand him? But we know at once that there is the Badness—and it is music!

There is the element of Badness in me.

I long to cultivate my element of Badness. Badness compared to Nothingness is beautiful. And so, then, I wait also for some one to come over the hill with things other than Happiness. But whatever I wait for, nothing comes.

## L'envoi: October 28, 1901

And so there you have my Portrayal. It is the record of three months of Nothingness. Those three months are very like the three months that preceded them, to be sure, and the three that followed them—and like all the months that have come and gone with me, since time was. There is never anything different; nothing ever happens.

Now I will send my Portrayal into the wise wide world. It may stop short at the publisher; or it may fall still-born from the press; or it may go farther, indeed, and be its own undoing.

That's as may be.

I will send it.

What else is there for me, if not this book?

And, oh, that some one may understand it!

—I am not good. I am not virtuous. I am not sympathetic. I am not generous. I am merely and above all a creature of intense

passionate *feeling.* I feel—everything. It is my genius. It burns
me like fire.—

My Portrayal in its analysis and egotism and bitterness will
surely be of interest to some. Whether to that one alone who may
understand it; or to some who have themselves been left alone; or
to those three whom I, on three dreary days, asked for bread, and
who each gave me a stone—and whom I do not forgive (for that is
the bitterest thing of all): it may be to all of these.

But none of them, nor any one, can know the feeling made of
relief and pain and despair that comes over me at the thought of
sending all this to the wise wide world. It is bits of my wooden
heart broken off and given away. It is strings of amber beads
taken from the fair neck of my soul. It is shining little gold coins
from out of my mind's red leather purse. It is my little old life-
tragedy.

It means everything to me.

Do you see?—It means *everything* to me.

It will amsue you. It will arouse your interest. It will stir your
curiosity. Some sorts of persons will find it ridiculous. It will
puzzle you.

But am I to suppose that it will also awaken compassion in
cool, indifferent hearts? And will the sand had barrenness look so
unspeakably gray and dreary to coldly critical eyes as to mine?
And shall my bitter little story fall easily and comfortably upon
undisturbed ears, and linger for an hour, and be forgotten?

Will the wise wide world itself give me in my outstretched
hand a stone?

THE END

MARY MACLANE   "I find myself at this stage of womankind and
nineteen years, a genius, a thief, a liar—a general moral vagabond, a
fool more or less, and a philosopher . . ." (1901) Mary MacLane was a
solitary eccentric born in 1881 in Canada and lived her entire life in

Butte, Montana. She harbored literary ambitions at an early age, and a small publisher in Chicago published her diaries, *The Story of Mary MacLane, by Herself*, in 1902, from which this text is excerpted. This afforded Mary some little fame (she made a brief trip to New York City), which she craved, but like Emily Dickinson, hers was a loner's soul. She published a novel in 1903 and another memoir in 1917 and, in 1929, Mary MacLane died as she lived, alienated and alone in Butte.

# HENRY DARGER

In the presence of such fearful disaster there are many persons, even among the most devout religious, even Catholics who do and will say, but also there are some who will think that this in some manner a visitation decreed upon the communities which suffer for our Short comings before God,

The very magnitude and super human force of it will suggest to many minds the thought of an ordered punishment and warning for offenses against a higher power.

Yet such a concept happily more rarely held now than in earlier times is of course revolting to sober judgement and to the instincts of all religious reverance.

For it would imply that countless multitudes of the innocent should suffer indescribable cruelty it would attempt the impossible feat of justifying the smiting of these four big towns where all the inhabitants lived lives of peaceful helpful industry, mostly Catholic of like population, very religious, children brought up the way they should go and the sparing of communications and communities where no man or woman served the gods of dishonest wealth and wicked slothful vicious idleness. Children were from far away places were sent to that convent, because the nuns there knew how to bring up and train children, the way these children were in that Convent youd a believe they were already Saints.

And also this was no vengeance decreed for human Short comings. God does not make or order disasters. And neither does the devil though it is said he has the power to do so.

God wont let him. No sir—ee. These disasters are superhuman but not supernatural. It was but a manifestation of the very unchangeable irresistible forces of nature governed by physical laws which are inexorable. To blame God for this disaster would be rank rash blasphemy.

Nature knows neither revenge nor pity. Old Mother Nature does not select her victims, nor does she turn aside to save the good who are in her path. Besides powerful as Mother Nature is she cannot prevent what is going to happen.

The most powerful twister, hurricane, thunderstorms, big blizzards and freeze rains cannot make themselves turn off their course or come head on. She no matter what she is going to do cannot stop herself. And as her concern is not with all persons but with the race so she is moved not by mercy but by law. Mother Nature has to obey the natural law. There is no way out for her.

To the limited vision of man with his brief life Mother Nature seems incredibly cruel heartless and destructive and wasteful beyond comprehension. Her teachings may be learned at the most fearful costs. Us men will ask ourselves what lessons are taught by this overwhelming sacrifice.

There is made plain first the immitability of natural laws of Mother Nature and the utter powerlessness of man when he pits his strength against their full demonstration. It is revealed again that old Mother Nature has forces which before all the might of human intellect remain absolutely unconquerable.

But there flowed from an awful catastrophe as this a brighter and better influence than this.

With all its horror and shock there came a great joining of minds and hearts.

The whole world felt the thrill of kinship and humanity.

For the time being all conception of social caste and class distinction the most unworthy thoughts of beings fashioned all in the image of their maker are leveled or even forgotten.

Indifference and selfishness disappear. Thoughout the nation throughout the world there thrills the uplifting current of brotherhood the consciousness that we be of one blood.

Specifically does not such an appalling event serve to awaken responsibility among the wealthy and powerful twards the poor and the weak. When all goes well when there are no thunderous warnings such as this of the helplessness of man against the forces of Old Mother arrayed against him, the fortunate do not realize that for millions mere existance is a most poignant struggle that hunger and cold and disease prevail when there are no ghastly tornados or floods, or unusally severe heat or cold to make them (. . .) and pictureque.

We do not doubt that there are many who were stirred by the shock of this dreadful story to a deeper and more sympathetic understanding with the conditions that now surround them on every side.

If any further good can from a catastophe so cruel it ought to be in the stimulating pride of race which it engenders,

Such experiences have a unique effect upon the American people. Yet this calamity was so great, so overwhelming that there seemed no rebound. How could it. The population of Zaneville, and Chestershire totally wiped out and the towns too. Chester town also wiped out in property and heading the death and injured and refugee list.

Though this record breaking disaster destruction and hardship did open great reservoirs of latent energy interventive and enterprise, what could it do. All bridges gone field wiped out roads torn up to be almost impassable there was the block.

Chester town overwhelmed by this convulsion of Old Mother Nature seems apparently doomed to moulder away in forgotten ruin no one around to clear the wreck and a chance to build a greater city than before. It did in later years be restored but very very little.

And what ever restoration there was, was only in the territory where the 31 buildings were missed by the twister.

Calamity sets free such a flow of creative power that destruction itself usually only makes progress. Will it do there in the future. Im afraid never. The engineer and fireman agreed with me. These disasters usually concentrate upon constructive enterprize, and only stores of emotional energy that in other times are expanded in the fierce struggle of competitive existance.

Galveston suddenly overwhelmed by a terrific storm and the sea apparantly was doomed forever, but her people cleared the wreck and built a greater city than before.

Before the ashes of destroyed San Francisco had cooled, the vision of a better community rose before the work of her people and they made it real.

Can that be done here? I hardly do not believe that man kind that by the power of God that man is humbled because man will not be humbled . . .

HENRY DARGER    Born in Brazil in 1892, Darger spent most of his life in Illinois. He lived for 40 years in a single room in Chicago, working by day as a janitor in a hospital, and by night on his 19,000 page magnum opus, begun in 1916 at age 24: "The Adventures of the Vivian Girls in What is Known as the Realms of the Unreal or the Glandelinian War Storm or the Glandico–Abiennian Wars, as caused by the Child Slave Rebellion." The text excerpted here was taken from this unique masterpiece, not found until after his death in 1972.

# SWITZERLAND

## TESTAMENT

In the name of both, above mentioned and below signed, in future, almighty reigning instances, the holy Saint Adolf, Great-Great-God and author of the book, as well as the holy Saint Mary, Great-Great-Goddess, all musical and geographical, 13 books, piled up in this hospital-cell and, made by myself, should be printed at an excellent Swiss printing workshop, altogether, a total of 16,500,000,000, copies or volumes, and be bound nice and elegant, at a ditto, bookbinder, with the simple and excellent title - the Holy St. Adolf, II. and then, at the selling-price, per individual copy, of 16 Fr. 50 Rappen, in retail, wholesale and world trade, each, be presented to the purchaser. The fixed income of all these volumes, would then be, altogether, about 272,250,000,000, Fr., of which, circa, about 25,000,000,000, francs, would fall to the share of bookprinter, bookbinder and transport-costs. The fixed, absolute net profit of this printing result would then be, all together, 252,250,000,000, Fr., of which I above mentioned and below signed, to the high, Swiss Federal Council, about: 2,000,000,000, Fr. in most legal and most excellent information do testamentarily bequeath, for the respective use of building, formation and excellent repair of different generally useful and charitable foundations and their excellent financing, etcetera: not only in the Canton of Berne: no!! In all, individually, highly special Swiss Cantons: as well as the odd, 250,000,000, Fr., for the excellent distribution amongst the poor, sick and needy, each, of my beloved, Swiss-Country.(. . .)

Respectfully signs, greets and concludes, my humble self, St. Adolf the II, Great-Great-God. Berne, 1916.

TRANSLATED BY ANNE-MARIE THALMANN

It should however, still be mentioned here that, in 1868, together with my very own parents and brothers and sisters as well as with their numerous friends, relations and acquaintances and directly accompanied by God, the Allmighty Fatther, I climbed right to the very highest altitude of the 995 hours high Siiriuss-Rage on the planet of the same name on a gigantic Sorrantton (Heavenly Paradise-Bird) but during the descent, from approximately half the height: Which means from definitely no less than about: 485 hours,* I fell down the glittering, glistening rock face, which at this point juts out rather strongly, only to be snatched right out of mid-air down below and thus saved by a hard-working, deft giant cellar worker whom God the Allmighty Fatther had Personally alarmed and drawn his attention to me. O, how I wish that, under the very own miraculous guidance of God the Allmighty Fatther I could see everything once more, yes, really everything which I saw, lived through, suffered and experienced on the whole of the Globe, yes, even in quite a considerable part of the whole, immeasurable Universe, during those approx. 6 years from 1864, the year of my birth, until 1870: With the exception of those innumerable, mainly gigantic catastrophes. O time of youth, o happy time. (1913)

*1 hour = approx. 5000 m.

TRANSLATED BY KIKO GASKELL AND PETER JONES

There! And now I see and hear quite clearly before my eyes, quite a few meters above the ground, a lovely wonderful angel who, with well-sounding voice, speaks these words: Halleluiah! Glory to God! Amen! Amen! Shortly after I stumbled over a root and fell down. Alright!! At the time I was only 3 years old. And now I hear quite clearly in front of me a voice in the air: A-ha! Now E's a Monkey! Alright!! The voices in the air increased and now, in the Half-Moon shaped, wood-enclosed, Fairy-Like side bay of afforesaid wood gully at the entrance of which aforesaid Trikandero was situated, I saw quite clearly about more than about a dozen of the most charming, graceful angels of male and female sex with the following well rhymed utterances: The Angels' Voices in the Oak Glade! Sent by God to the Oron Shade. Halleluia. 1,867.

TRANSLATED BY KIKO GASKELL AND PETER JONES

---

The positions of the numerals up to the miriaads. Signed, Doufi.
1. One, ten, hundred.
2. One-thousand, ten-thousand, hundred-thousand.
3. One-million, ten-million, hundred-million.
4. One-milliard, tenmilliard, hundred-milliard.
5. One-billion, tenbillion, hundred-billion.
6. One-billiard, tenbilliard, hundred-billiard.
7. One-trillion, ten-trillion, hundredtrillion.
8. One-trilliard, ten-trilliard, hundred-trilliard.
9. One-quadrillion, ten-quadrillion, etc.
10. One-quadrilliard, tenquadrilliard, etc.
11. One-Regoniff, tenregoniff, etc.
12. One-Suniff, tensuniff, etc.
13. One-Jeratiff, tenjeratiff, hundred-jeratiff.
14. One-Unitif, ten-Unitif, etc.
15. One-Vidoniss, ten-Vidoniss, etc.
16. One-Weratif, ten-Weratif, etc.
17. One-Hylotif, ten-Hylotif, etc.

18. One-Ysantteron, ten-Ysanterron, etc.
19. One-Zernantt, ten: Zernannt, etc.
20. One-Agoniff, ten-Agoniff, etc.
21. One-Benitif, ten-Benitif, etc.
22. One Corrantt, ten-Korranntt, etc.
23. One-Deritif, ten-Deritif, etc.
24. One-Eratif, ten-Eratif, etc.
25. One Ferrantto, ten-Ferrantto, etc.
26. One-Geratif, ten-Geratif, etc.
27. One-Horatif, ten-Horatif, etc.
28. One-Inioth, ten-Inioth, hundred-Inioth.
29. One-Kariffa, ten-Kariffa, etc.
30. One-Legion, ten-Legion, etc.
31. One-Negrier, ten-Negrier, etc.
32. One Miriaad, ten-Miriaad, etc.
33. One Oberon, should not be exceeded, because same is a cat-tas-strophe. Hm!!

Indeed. Oberon, God of the Siirius-Hall-Giant-Foundation, Letter with a water-jet diameter of, 10,000 hours and, a height of about: 2220,000, hours, that is, hurled down direct from its summit-Giant-Town Mariposa, in Siirius-Hall-Fountain-Rage-Mariposa-Rage-Summit, Giant Town with 375,000,000 souls, that is, from its very highest altitude, precisely, about: 6,666,666 hours, and 6,666 feet high, and because of that, the positions of the numerals could not be increased and, multiplied any more. Alright!! The position of the miriaads amounts to the number of the staars, in the atzure blue firmament. But the position of Oberon amounts to everything which has any name at all on the latter. The very highest number of the Negrier, that means, 999,000,000,000,000,000,000,000,000,000,000,000,000,000,000 000,000,000,000,000,000,000,000,000,000,000,000,000,000, Ninehundred-andninetynine Negrier, alright!! Exactly for this blue number, my very own, most loved mother has bought direct and throughout, paid in cash, partly from earthly sovereigns, descended from various cong-gregations, regentts and chief-regentts, as well as, ditto, from innumerable, official, minor and major official regencies, of numerous satellites, Werrantts, Zionists, Corrintts, fixed stars, Ignotts, Negrantts, Polligohns, planets, regentts, ancestors, Hyloths, Ysahrs and Zornantts,* et-cettera. Alright!! God the Allmighty Father, accompanied all of us Swiss huntsmen and *Natuhrvorscher*, as well as their children, friends male and female, on his 5 very smallest satellites, Kondoor, Agralong, Kormora, Horatora, and Albatros, away from our earthly existence direct through the endless ether, through a great part of the whole universe, putting us down direct on numerous heavenly bodies of different kinds, as for example on the Moon and the Sun: Alright!!

*Zorn = rage, anger.

TRANSLATED BY KIKO GASKELL AND PETER JONES

---

Allgebrah:
   ?You don't say!! What does that mean; O, how fine is the Föhn.
   Answer: Allgebrah is Music! Is that soh!
   That's it: And for Every Instrumenntt.
   Anything visible or invisible to the Human Eye: Can be transformed by means of the well-educated human mind, goodwill, hard work and existing, suitable matterial into Music-Song-Text and that goes for the smallest to the biggest object or nonobject.
   Der Dicht'r reimt den Text in Strophen: Tohnsetzer setzt den Tohn.
   Beim Liebchen möcht ich einmal schlafen; Nun geht Es flugs dafon.

Und kommt der Böse mit den Schofen; So ist nur schuld der Sohn.

Der Guhte fürchtet sich vor Strofen! Und auch vor Spott und Hohn.

Drumm geht Er auch dafon.

Wandering diletannts! Piano virtuosos! Orchestras! Bands! the wanderer on the road! The oragnist and all the schools! From infants' school to High School: In short! All of them honor Allgebra, an old but Glorious invention of the Moorish peoples.? How many a beautiful: song uplifting heart and mind: has sounded, from days of old: out of the throats of well-trained choruses. Choirs of all kinds: Young people in their schoolrooms, the worker in the field: the cowherd high up on the alp and only a few days ago, I heard out of the atmosphere the merriest yodelling from the gondola of a balloon. Verily! Everyone happy and of good cheer. But a song is sung also at the sickbed of gravely ill or dying human beings, a comforting song is quietly, gently and ever quietly sung.? How often is a sinner who meets his fellow-creature at work, in the house or in the street, warned by soft sounds of his fellow-man's: Which however seldom finds its desired echo and dully, shyly, yes, often even with mocking mien the Shepherd drops you, to tinsel, poison and ridicule.

Erschreken heisst, ich sah den Geist, doch nicht auf rechten Weegen. Und wenn Er beisst, ei nun das weist, verlierst Du Gottes, Seegen. And now, dear fellow-humans: The voice of God is a human voice and is called Allgebrah.

Allgebra is music and song. May it be your sincerest endeavor forever and at all times to foster these gifts of God, to strengthen and ennoble them. God grant it!

Amen! Manual.

TRANSLATED BY KIKO GASKELL AND PETER JONES

. . . and, endless eternity is, neither round nor square, has absolutely no limits. On a stretch of absolutley not less than about: 420,000,000 German miles or 1,680,000,000 hours along which, in 1868, with my very own beloved parents, brothers and sisters, friends, under the constant presence of God Almighty the Fatther, I travelled in the infinite spaces of creation by the most manyfold means of transport, as for instance: Gigantic and majestic carrier, luxury and, transport birds, island-mothships, giant-foundations, lightning-serpents, omnipotence-moths, etcettera, etcettera, always in quite comfortable riding informattion, I saw during every staar-bright night a chaos of staars of the most manyfold kinds such as the most skilful writer's hand is absolutely unable to describe and to explain. Indeed, God is good, omniscient, all-wise, all-merciful, omnipotent, and, his omnipotence, has no limits. Yes, I saw with my own eyes, By his powerful wonder word: Let there be: the creation of things which would, quite energetically deign to defy description. And now, one should still do a bit of *"vöögeln"** but, in this text, I am not exactly a master at it. Appropo: The blue birds; The green birds; The orange birds; The red birds; The black birds; Hm!! They have many colors. Ha, ha, ha, ha. Alright!! I start small and, climb ever higher. But today I've had a fall, therefore the children bawl. The birds: Well, yes, I too have *gevöögelt* now and then: In our neighborhood they are certainly not of enormous size. And to characterize on the spot their various names which, after all, every child here knows rather exactly, would cost me too much, time, trouble and paper, and so I will start with the explanation of the many different flyers in the high southern zones and eternal snow regions, on the southern and southeastern part of our globe. Luxury and cage-birds. The Kaiser organ; The Gold Cock; The Sickel: The Dolphins: The Pheasant: The Pelican: The Rummel: The Ostrich: Etcettera: Are on the conttinentt Southmeridian, on the Great-East Sea, Brand Sea and Pacific Ocean islands, as well as the gigantic Swan, The Goose, The Duck, The Chicken and, manyfold, partly, gigantic pigeons, etcettera, not only because of their highly valuable plumage, and Their eggs: But also because of their highly tasty meat, (comestibles) are highly useful, and in afforesaid parts of the world, present in enormous numbers. Let us now turn, to the numerous birds of prey, which are, in those parts, in some places present in quite enormous numbers, and, are for man, animal and also for the lesser sorts of their own kind, in the highest degree, harmful, troublesome, and dangerous. There are, for the huntsman and gun, in the first place The Condoor: The Agralong: The Murvitt: The Muhrfrison: The Printtong: The Horatoos: The King: The Kaiser: The Duke: The Prince: The Knight: The Graph: The Master: The Menelik: The Sartoos: And many others more: Most of them of gigantic size. Oh yes: didn't all the Swiss-Avanttgaarde of huntsmen and *Natuhrvorscher* ride Anno 1868 on the great East Sea on the majestic back of a gigantic Horatoos for no less than a distance of 280 hours from the Djungle Giant Island as far as the giant town of Wangen, 186,000,000 souls in the Fattherwood district along the Southmeridian east coast as comfortably and without danger as in the most elegantt cab on land. But apart from that, the afforesaid giant birds are the most pecuniary robbers of The whole Southern and Southeastern Conttinentt. And now we come straight to the manyfold load, luxury and satellite birds of the extreme Southeast, on our planet, Earth. And that which is not, May it soon be. Ha, ha, ha. ?How: ?Would you, kind reader, like to stage with me a majestic voyage, as far as or to the very farthest heavenly bodies in the realm of The divine Universe: So

kindly accompany me by ship, vehicle and railway, to the gigantic God-Fatther-Heaven Island, in the Southern part of the
immense, almost endless, Great-East-Sea. Ha, ha, ha. Starting
from Corpse-Rage-East or, Sun-Rage-East, two respectable giant
towns on the Southeasterly part of the Southmeridian or, St.
Adolf Continentt, travelling Eastward in a rather straight line
over the great East Sea, we now come straight into the harbor of
God-Father-Heaven-Hall, the giant town numbering a little
over 80,000,000 souls. And, after a short inspection of afforesaid
giant town and Its, majestic surroundings, we now go on by
vehicle, or train, straight over the greatest part of afforesaid
island South coast, past numerous great and giant towns, villages, places and market towns, through the most manyfold
forest plantations, gaardens, woods, meadows and promenades
towards God-Fatther-Heaven-Serpent-Hall, the giant town,
which, Today, Anno 1913, counts a little over 100,000,000 souls.
Alright!! After reciprocal Rundetzvaus and manyfold discussions,
explanations and, arguments with the supreme authority there,
you will immediately find them prepared to arrange the journey
to the very furthest heavenly bodies on gigantically majestic
carrier and transport giant birds, in the presence, of God the
Almighty Fatther as long as you are all ready to serve the Latter
and be devoted to Him with all your heart, body and soul. Holy
cow: Gigantic, scintillating Allbatross: ditto, Kormanntts: ditto,
Ferantoo's, Garnie, Kolang and Muralt-Giant-Transport-Birds
carry Altogether our manyfold travel utensils, as well as the
whole, enormous, Swiss-Avanttgaarde of huntsmen and *Natuhrvorscher*, with numerous, actiive and passiive members, among
them of course also the extremely pretty, youthful Highness, Princess Amalia of, God-Fatther-Heaven-Serpent-Hall: And, after already having in every detail investigated and inspected innumerable of the most many fold staars, we find ourselves, without

knowing how, on the Quarantt Heaven, in God's holy halls. And so on. Song, in honor of the afforesaid, charming and gracious princess, Amalia of G.F.H.Sp.Hall. . . .

*vogeln* is slang for sexual intercourse.

TRANSLATED BY KIKO GASKELL AND PETER JONES

## LETTERS OF ADOLF WÖLFLI

Waldau near Berne, the 22nd of April 1905

Esteemed sister-in-law.

I find it necessary to give the following reply to the recently received letter. I was happy to hear from you again: Regret however very much, that you are suffering from a sick leg. I wish you a speedy recovery. Since the 4th of June, 1895, I am now accomodated in the psychiatric clinic Waldau, because I was frightened by my own beloved, whom I intended to marry. Unfortunately, I let her go again and the consequence was that we were both arrested. Of course, I started to yell and kick up a row, which is usually the case in such circumstances. Since then I am lying here, most horribly sick, in the midst of terrible noise and screaming, and can no longer regain force. I think I will die soon. Try again once more dear sister-in-law, to visit me as soon as possible and if possible to bring along a small pack of tobacco and 1 or 2 pencils. I am always drawing. But do not forget on any account, to take along little Emma and if possible brother Johann. I want to finish with friendly greetings.
Adolf Wölfli.
Motto. Go get gabbage gobbets. (Ggabis-Ggope ggaufen gefalligst)

Waldau, the 5th of September, 1907.

Esteemed sister-in-law,

To pass the time I have now taken up writing. However, no longer for all Seven. And even if I did much wrong, that will soon be forgotten. Supposedly, I squashed the North Pole and cut Europe in two. Oh what rubbish. Lick the sandstone wall. Scold over 1000 sticks. That surely is a torture. Farewell oh vale of tears!

However, that won't last forever Mother. Then he pulls hard, your good one. And the blood is pink. Tomorrow we are all dead.

Death penalty, follows accident or adultery. Ittem: It will be something like it. Then I don't know how to help myself anymore. I was never mentally and physically as stupid as now. Nowhere is peace to be had. And were I in Affghanistahn, it would still be magalomaniac, to be thinking of trifles, for I must direct everything. Cheers—New Year.

They are building a lot here in the Waldau: The devil knows what is to become of it. Probably the city of Berne is already spreading out towards our area. Anyway: there will probably soon be 100,000 inhabitants. A propos: Only very talented gymnasts can fly backwards on a broom. Wa: Such color in the face: That will be a severe supreme penal court. Good-bye, my love: Good-bye. And, how are you in Wattenwyl: Are you well, I think you could soon dare to come visit me again. Even if I am the stupid clown, something nevertheless comes to my mind, I will always, go on drawing diligently. And if everything falls to pieces, Even the thunder rumbles: I wish my dear one a good night, and throw myself into the Aaar. Then I'm thirsty.

For sure the mentally ill are insolent. They can do nothing but quarrel without end. Where does dear God live, Down There. And so go with Him, down there. And lock yourself in the chamber. Fear and pain, thus pass on. Dear sister-in-law, if possible, come and see me soon. Next Sunday my brother Johann is probably coming. I enticed him with a self-made picture, in fact the most beautiful I've ever made. What happens to my order now. I've only pains to handle. The old bear died: before 120, candles. Now the lion is Lucerne, studious by day and by night. He still goes on loving her, on his warm cushion.

With friendly greetings from your brother-in-law Adolf, Pattient.

(Letter to the "Printing Workshop Wiss, Gurtengasse")
Mental Asylum Waldau near Berne, the 7th of April, 1912

Dear Sir.

Below-signed asks you in all politeness, whether you might be willing to print, within the shortest period, till circa May 14, 1912, circa, alright: Strong, 35 pounds or, 17½ kilos worth-writings, with over 700, mostly beautiful wood engraving, steel engraving and copper engraving-hand-drawings, many, mostly music compositions and dance-songs with text, testament-disclosures with rough calculations of interest remarks, many prayers, etcettera. All 17½ kilogr. bonds, presented in very amusing and instructive fashion, one and all, include highly personal adventures experienced during the time of our scientific research work in the years, 1864 to 1872, and, represent in 5 big Heftern a total-estimate-worth of at least, 34,000 Fr. I would be disposed, to have 75,000 copies printed, at my own cost and risk, the copy at the price of 1 Fr. 20 Rp., with the title: (Scientific geographical voyages of the Swiss Highness Helveetia, on the planet, Earth.) Well, well: But she isn't doing it quite right. A propos: Great-bombs and elements-thunder and lightening: That's not really what I meant. Alright! Please. But I can't go on. So: Once printed all 75,000 copies, should be immediately given to an expert, to an efficient bookbinder, to be, nicely, bound, straight away. The money for both payments, is kept here on the spot. However, please do not let the whole story get too expensive for my sake. And, kindly see to it, or, if you do not have time, maybe the bookbinder, that all 75,000 volumes or, copies, are put on sale, sure and correct, as quick as possible. The entire, obtained capital of about: 90,000 Fr. should then be sent, post restant, to the following address. Mr., Adolf Wölfli, Delinquent by misfortune of the V. men's department, Mental Asylum Waldau near Berne. Direction, von Speyer. The 17½ kilogram scientific and geographical bonds should, however, as soon as you can print them, be collected, an errand-boy, from your very own printing workshop, etcettera, in so far as I should not be capable of coming to the city of Berne on foot today. Yes, I was frightened by God the holy Ghost: that is, by my most beloved darling and so, off with the little horns and dead. Signed, Respectfully, Adolf Wölfli from Schangnau.

Dear Sir. Please let me know as soon as possible how high the expenses will be for printing and binding and, whether the little book, nicely bound, with a picture of Her Swiss Highness, Helveetia with the federal coat of arms, can really be sold at the price of 1 Fr. 20 Rp. and, in wholesale and world trade.

Perhaps you know the book, given to the printing workshop Wiss in Langnau beginning of the seventies to be printed and bound, with the title, (From the Cradle to the Graave: Or, Through work and sweat, suffering and ordeals, and even through prayer into damnation. So: I am He, the innumerably mentioned Doufi. And today still, the youngest member of the Swiss Hunter and, Scientist-Gaarde, travelling over the entire earth in the years 1864 to 1870. Signed Respectfully Adolf Wölfli. Berne.

("The Schüpfen-Letter," 1922)

The Schüpfen-letter.? What's this all about!!!? What does it mean, for goodness sake. Now listen. From the hour of my birth on, March 1, 1,864: I travelled with all my family members and, over 5,000, male and female friends from our home and fatherland, from Switzerland, with the almighty family and its whole, gigantic, Travelling-Avantt-Gaarde, in not less than 10, each, separate Travelling periods, on its tremendous Travelling-Object, Giant-Lightening-Transparantt, in all directions of the Wind-Rose, from Star to Star, through the whole and entire, highly proper, old and, new, St. Adolf-Giant-Creation: As well as, a large part of the Endless and infinite, consisting of absolute, pure Nothing, eternity, at the occasion of which I saw, experienced and learnt much and, now one way, now another, had to endure, a total of over 10,000, fatal accidents: But the old Gods, is still alive. Although I was no fool: No: But as frightened and cheated casualty, right in it. Hm!! Apropos: There are more the likes of them: So. chirp: And also snore: D'rliih D'rlüüüüh D'zlüüüüü: And, Chchchchch: Chchchchch. Well now. I, for myself, have no time to sleep, during the day and, last summer when we absolved, a beautiful, quite amusing and funny trip, to the "Bären" in Schüpfen, I set my mind on drawing large and beautiful portraits, for the purpose of my earlier experiences and adventures, to be suited to the latter, which I have now succeeded, more or less well. The 10 commandments, from Africa. Of course: All, each, African views. And so I ask the highly honored "Bären"-innkeeper-family in Schüpfen, to frame the latter, each, nicely and without fault and then to hang them, on the walls of the ballroom. I send you these 10 pictures, as voluntary, gift. To cover further expenses for the latter, of course, for carpenter and glass cutter, etcettera: And, if possible, also, a gratuity for my effort and, the used material: I recommend you to organize a collection for voluntary donations, every time you have a dance: A marriage: A child-baptism: Or any other kind of happy celebration.? Why. That way you do not lose anything: And to some extent you would also do me a good turn. My advice is good and flawless: Believe me. But now, you should arrange it amongst yourself, to buy about 4 or 5, each, clean and fresh newspaper sheets, like this one here, in order to copy; That means, to write, the whole and entire text on the backside of the 10 portraits, each, according to their numbered order, as indicated below. This page presents the beginning or, the preface to the whole story. You should carefully, pfotograph all 10 pictures and, add these resulting, however, uncolored pictures, to your respective explanations. Actually, you yourself could write a short final chapter about my Humble Self and, about Kirch-Dorf and the community of Schüpfen, etcettera, (Don't forget the Turba-Moor!) So: Have this whole story, nicely together, printed perfectly in a printing workshop of the city of Berne and, you have a rather pretty and instructive, amusing little book, for old and young: rich and poor: sick and healthy: noble and common: And, for both sexes. With a nice, net profit. The latter should not be less than about: 165,000, francs. 15,000, Fr., will be needed to cover the expenses of editor, printer, binder and travelling salesman etcettera. Ha, ha, ha, ha, ha. And now you have, about: 150,000, francs, fixed and absolute net profit, to which I congratulate you with all my heart. Sacred thundering. Pong: Very good!! Rrrrrumm-ppedibumm. But now to the list of portraits: That is, their perfect numbering and, declared value of the individual copies, all together.

List of portraits: by, St. Adolf II., Berne.
Portrait Nr. 1, The latin a: Worth, 500, francs.
Nr. 2, The Rose-Garden-Ring: Worth, 550, francs.
Nr. 3, The latin flap: Worth, 450, francs.

Nr. 4, The Orange-Cup: Worth, 400, francs.
Nr. 5, The Cape Wood-Rose: Worth, 350, francs.
Nr. 6, The Teddy-Bear Small St. Adolf-Kiss: Worth, 450, francs.
Nr. 7, St. Adolf II. and the Rattlesnake: Worth, 550, francs.
Nr. 8, The Standard Telescope Stand: Worth, 500, francs.
Nr. 9, The Cape Wood-Lily: Worth, 500, francs.
Nr. 10, the latin Z, Worth, 450, francs.
Summa, all together, 4,700, Fr. or, together with text and letter, all pictures fixed with fine oil, about, pong: 5,000, francs, as estimation.

But, Sacred thundering: Yesterday was grand: Yesterday I and my father and three other strong men, threw out a sick little tailor: Uuuh! Did it scream. But I, booze a whole stable-bucket full, if it must be. Respectfully signs, greets and finishes my Humble Self, the Schüpfen-Peasant, St.Adolf II. or Wöulfli-Döufu. New Clinic, Waldau, Berne, 1,922.

COMPLIED BY ELKA SPOERRI    (Reprinted from *Adolf Wölfli* [Berne, 1976], with the kind permission of the Adolf Wölfli Foundation.)

ADOLF WÖLFLI    "Naturalist, poet, writer, draughtsman, composer, farm laborer, milker, handyman, gardener, plasterer, cemet-layer, rail worker, day-laborer, knife-grinder, fisher, boatman, hunter, migrant worker, grave-digger, and soldier of the Emmenthal Battalion, 3rd Company, 3rd Section. Alright!! St.Adolf II, Master of Algebra, Military Commander-in-Chief and Chief Music-Director, Giant-Theater-Director, Captain of the Almight-Giant-Steamship and Dr. of Arts and Sciences, Director of the Algebra-and-Geography-Folder-Fabrication and Hunting General. Inventor of 160 original highly valuable inventions patented for all times by the Russian Zar, and for ever the glorious victor of tremendous Giant-Battles."

Wölfli was born in 1864 in the Swiss canton of Berne. Orphaned at an early age he grew up as a farmhand, and was imprisoned for

attempted child molesting. He was finally committed to an asylum—
the Waldau, near Berne—for repeated arrests in 1895. Often violent,
Wölfli nonetheless began an intensive creative life of painting and
drawing, composing, and writing, cramming his cell with manuscripts
and drawings until his death in 1930.

## ALOÏSE CORBAZ

Lausanne, 4-28-1917

Your Majesty!

During my short stay in Berlin, I grew familiar with the
simplicity of an emperor whose throne would crush me if he
were not pious. Thus do I seek his indulgence to communicate
my thoughts to him frankly as to a dear confessor and protector
of Switzerland. Certain that we were spared the war, thanks be to
God, through the agency of your imperial benevolence, I cannot
restrain myself from expressing to you, with passion and the
profound and delerious joy of one rescued, my deep gratitude.
First of all I shall confide to you a great concern which touches
me personally: To fend off an epidemic of ever increasing unem-
ployment, Monsieur de Coppet, ex-president of the Swiss Con-
federation, has decided to create new industries to employ men
of all nationalities in our country. The temporary maintenance
of the military uniform workshops to be shut at the end of May,
will undertake, perhaps in the future, the outfitting of companies
subsidized by the State, in order to assist poverty-stricken women.

Allow me to recommend Monsieur de Coppet to your high
influence, as I am convinced that with one word you could
smooth out the difficulties he will encounter, totally lacking raw
materials Majesty with all my heart since this heavy and terrible

responsibilty for the world war has fallen on him. Imagining that you were forced by general incredulity from declaring it, I cast to all winds your old title of emperor of peace. You will probably be considered and fanatically loved as such.

As an antimilitarist I seek in vain to establish peace without the majority of humans being Christian. In granting nature's work in the mind, war remains in the mind. The splendid and perfect harmony of nature, produced by the sun originating from the vital center of the earth (I see but one planet, regardless of what the astronomers say, a single apple of divine love) in the cohesion of opposite factors, affords a glimpse of the Holy Spirit uniting good with evil to obtain light or the divine love that harmoniously fuses races, nations and religions in the peace of God that surpasses all intelligence. The first symbol of divine love is the gift of nature created by the great Clockmaker, said Voltaire. The second symbol is the gift of Christ, God manifest in the flesh. He is the way, the truth and the life: He shows us the way through parables put into practice literally and figuratively/ spiritually and materially/ on earth. The truth in mutual sacrifice thus plants in embryo the new birth in virtue so as to gain the promised land on earth, "peace." Life in the faith in one God of love, All-powerful, defender of right and justice on earth. I am amazed by divine love.

All's well that ends well

Eternal life in the resurrection of the soul in the bodies of our dearly beloved abandoned on earth; thus is eternal life transmitted from generation to generation on earth . . . A lasting peace could not have been established without the annihilation of the temples of sordid and vermilion gold, the pedestal of criminal human egotism, an idol adored instead and in place of the Creator-Saviour-Redeemer. Consequently, in order to be happy in the face of the collapse of earthly grandeurs, we must return to a Christian life, subject as we are—atheists included—to immutable divine laws, according to which we undoubtedly shall reap what we have sown.

If you happened to like suffering in rags You would inevitably be of the torches The third symbol of divine love is peace and those who procure it often at the cost of their whole life or their blood, to give birth to it one must lovingly sacrifice oneself. Soon no more Burdens. W. II speaks of Peace.

Picture illuminated by A divine inspiration
Since our childhood Of gratitude
To Christ the Saviour Whose Sacred Heart
By its sacrifice fecundates The world's soul

Why then in evoking your memory do I vibrate like a bell announcing the nuptials of angels? slowly dying of an ineffable love inspired in me by your splendid gaze met by chance at the Potsdam encounter in 1913. You were sparkling from head to toe, deified by the sublime beaming of your dear face.

Humbly I lower my eyes
Your dazzling gaze leaves
A noble and sacred impression
Profound pure and azure
Upon my heart
Its majestic sweetness
Seals my soul for life
Oh! my God! I'm overjoyed.

The impulse of this enchantment brings me devoutly to my knees behind the door through which you have disappeared

O pain! O despair! I shall not succeed in grasping the delicate flowers with penetrating scents that you involuntarily deposited in each recess of my heart immured in suffering. Would that I could temper my soul again in fire, in the star-studded heavenly eyes of an inaccessible man whom I love so madly. Only a miracle of divine love could raze the walls that eternally separate me from this love. Overwhelmed, kissing the cold flagstones

before the altar of Lord Jesus I beseech him to intercede with
God the Father, with thanksgivings, so that he may banish any
danger that threatens you. In Sans-Souci park, always and still
now an adorable feminine apparition follows me and deliciously
envelops me in her marvelous smile (like a spring breeze) which
cured my nostalgia. I see her in dreams as an eagle-dove soaring
ideally rose as the Empress of German peace on the precious
head of Your Majesty the emperor of peace, Wilhelm II:
Heaven and earth shall pass away
But my words shall not pass away
Matthew 24.55

Seek out my soul in your large eyes
Where the firmament studded with stars of the heavens is
    mirrored
Rest, for a moment at least, my wet gaze
On this fine-featured face stamped with majesty
Amazing and adorable fictive apparition
Which makes [my soul] languid and pensive
This cloud streaked white blue and rose
Softly kisses the gloomy earth.
In reflecting you the vastness of the oceans
Sees its entrails purged of hell
The rock caressed by the trembling wave
Ransacks the dishevelled vermilion cloud
Celebrates with delight the door to heaven
Slowly effaces the bitterness of spleen
O miraculous nature, divine school
Take form, give me your obol!
Whether you wish it or not, in spite of you
In suffering your soul is mine
Says the Almighty creator, Saviour
My love sends you Christ the Redeemer

## MARY STUART IN THE AUKENTHALER
## BOARDING SCHOOL

The bouquet of the squier Villepreux his diamond head of the artist Knie the two spouses at the foot of the Kervadec cross came from the balcony of Genevieve from Candia The hummingbird and the great Pardon of Ploermel [opera] all the newlyweds joined hands at church [she bore the name of rose on her forehead wreathed with veils] they had Byron's intuition to have encountered their beloved angels in the outline of orange blossoms with their dress as white as a great flower of the Siegesallee of Sans Souci in a necklace of the pearl-rose of India [in her imperial crown] to kiss the Marble statues in the bed of roses or a monument on them [in carrying it several students] from Montreux on the altar—or on her beautiful ship of love (of the black or white swan) of the beautiful blue Danube blue horizons [Hotel] of her great blue eyes Istenvelled azcrett angylom— vanquished before this marble O Vesta I raised your nuptial veils finery of England florid Elizabeth. When the hummingbird sings through the windows they carry off his bride on purpose to conceal from you the fleur-de-lys butterfly on purpose for you the roses open on the balcony [of the Walewska woman Mary Louise] in the mantle fallen from her onto me I hear her sing atala [lying down like an orchestra conductor] in the imperial mantle—Wagner's Walkyrie. He will raise his kneeling royal head to the nude she-devil's foot in the purple mantle begs me to marry him [or Siegfried in the moonlight surrounded by amaryllis flowers] lying on his graciella in the Polo grotto like the Axenstrasse grotto of the magic fairy great butterfly when Hella lifts up her veils or the wings of the thousand-colored air. he lays out Fernand his brocaded mantle on Cypris' bed. with an angel in the bed sky of Marie Antoinette. They have the queen of England leaning on her elbows in Napoleon's triple-crowned bed stretched out like Marceau - half dead in love with her - on the contrary he is at the foot of the white mare has a broken back, as a sculptor of the queen Zita decorated with rare feathers and calasin the unfastened ruby mantle. and the veil and the gold and diamond diadem collyrium of a wedding box that composes the carriage of the newlyweds rush off or in the world the (final) bouquet in the world as a memory of a flower gathered in the flower crowd in offering Saint-Rosaire multitarts. the card game foresaw the nuptial bed of Marguerite of Burgundy. give me the second sleeve of the thrones or I'll make you leave the Pierrefontaine boarding house—O Marguerite marry me as a Venetian doge I shall carry you in my hands in my royal court mantle pluck the rose of Naples on two pontifical Holy See on the mediterranean Lido—All is light in their neon sign = Licht of Brodway. Christmas of the three Magi—

Francis Carco: I give you this florid corner these light blossoming trees this Helle-Paris mist that is lit Under these white and grey clouds. Easter procession [in white]. in Spain sleeping Sedia of angels carried by the popes of the faithful Preraphaelites of monuments . . .

They exchanged as lovers' gifts a colored egg in a necklace he adorned them with amorous devises—Christmas of the three Magi—This morning I ran into the train of the three great kings beneath the grand highway first I saw the bodyguards all gilded on their justaucorps the flags that were certainly very beautiful in the wind served as entertainment The camels which were certainly very beautiful carried brand new jewels [and the queen of Sheba Esther's tarts] and the drums with which to honor [repeat] from time to time rumbled their roll struck up the march each in turn In a chariot gilded all over [repeat] (of the Good Child) One saw the kings as modest as angels—One saw rich standards shine One heard sweet-voiced oboes [repeat] which from my God proclaimed the praises that told the songs with an admirable choice of a Christmas wedding. Astounded to hear this I drew aside to see the retinue Farther and farther away I have always followed them the shining star that led them [repeat] stopped short when it came to the Child. Next they entered to adore their king [repeat] on two knees they began their prayer And recognized his divine law—first Gaspard presents the gold [repeat] and My God you are the only king of glory And say everywhere that he comes to chase death away As a present Melchior offers the incense [repeat] telling him you are the god of armies [royal earth immense monstrance] saying you are the king and you are god all together Poverty humility [repeat] does not prevent your Divinity As for me I cry for it The poverty humility of your love are the certain proof As for me I cry for it my good God in sobbing I offer to you myrrh (of marriages) As for me to think of it I am more dead than alive one day for us on a cross of organ players—[without the radio of the Royal Biograph] As a mortal shall you end your sufferings You must die for the salvation of all—while listening to their organ concerts—

See the children—here's the Christmas celebration it's New Year's Day to play each one gets ready See what power winter has over nature threw down his [Imperial] mantle. No more flowers no more grass. And yet its beautiful [this husband of Hermine] . . . Christian midnight is a solemn time . . . as of yore a brilliant star brought from the orient the Magi Mistral and Mireille Spanish Toreros costume: We are in April the meadows grow green the almond trees are covered with white and pink flowers—the Alpilles like a gilded granite plinth in the blue sky—[How] its human ice-floe face of Napoleon standing over the world. the yawning people cannot keep silent Arms raised they presented to earth [when shall I have it all in bloom] their newborn son One would have thought the Welkerschlacht or the plinth in Siegesallee like a mysterious beacon calm glides in the skies Madame de Stael danced around like a fallen Liberty in the Welkerschlacht-basket filled with almond-tree roses the purple and gold lantern helmet in the setting sun the great Campeador general disarmament (all that remains is a review of the final banquet and bouquet) caught like a modern Joan of Arc [the red Catherine on horseback] naked in the cords of the brocaded banner—inclusively—in long folds trailing like a crown of banners—Like Herod's belt of bright purple laced into ribbons of the 7 natural wonders of the ancient worlds rolling inside at his feet the organ player and his book of Operas where these 7 Wonders in a book of love [atop the Larousse Bible] represent the hours of Gounod the composer: Mireille. Sapho Faust. Romeo and Juliette Philemon and Baucis. (Illumination of the creation for the city of lights of Brodway—Come back Jerusalem all lit up like Piccadilly.—the city of roses—Copenhagen. Ouchy bouquet of Bengali wiles. The book of the romaunt of the rose Hymn to Mary or Ave-Maria of Gounod—di lampe de Veneti the pope in his mantle The queen of Carthage— [child's swing] the queen of Sheba the queen Esther-Jezebel Pharaoh's daughter—The queen Victoria rose in diadem—The Empress Elizabeth—The Empress Eugenia—and her necklace of Chateaux of Queen Bertha Opera Sphinx Victoria-Cleopatra—Iphegenia in Aulis—a siren on the banks of the blue Nile— a true baluster as necklace—of the Capitol—The Composer Gounod—Romeo and Juliette—Faust his necklace of pink pearls from India Sapho her bouquet on the orange blossom bed—Werther marriage in the auto orchid bouquet of Pregny Rosia—[. . .]—Wilhelm II Iphegenia in Aulis many ballets and singer Jenny Lindt [they throw flowers there]—Walkyria Ave Maria—6 airs—Mme Lohengrin Zita remains on her feet with her ship as a wedding present it fell in her long mantle in removing it in a luxuriously furnished grotto—Disembarking of Cythera torch of the blond angel Gambetta in the arms of the general the headquarters on its knees—She also seemed like an angel of white marble from Easter processions in Spain—the white-eagled ones very high up like the sails of a ship by the painter boucher—seemed as well like a torch of the wonders of the world in her nuptial veils—in her Imperial Madame de Stael mantle (the universe belongs to her Weltall dir gesehen R Napoleon ihr gedenk—Delphine Corinne of Germany—the angel is found in the name of Charlemagne and his numismatic Madonnas [7 crowns of the 7 wonders of the ancient world]—a great European lady—and her gigantic purple awning on Versailles French Russian and Vaudois at Caux—on the palace of the Kremlin Alexandra—on the Rumine Palace seems like an icefloe standing over Egypt is covered with the crown of banners and the giant flag with 12 red stripes and 48 stars on the furthest point of the Capitol bursts (or bursting) in the wind of Atlantis—his elephant portico where the mahadrajah descends from the heights of his throne of Dehli many pachiderms lie down under the roma and stand up bronze hurling into space the victory chariots and his golden lamp suspended in the azure Chinese banners the sphinx of the [. . .] painted inside while engarlanding Bonaparte and his heraldic chariots Helvetic flowers bloom beneath the cloak of the Empress Elizabeth [atop the Larousse] on the altar of the fatherland Switzerland to Montre (ux) of goldwatch of vineyards planted in archangel flowers of Saint Light marches like a cignia and silver cup like angel waterlily with its wings in the air this peerless flower from angsoka [with marble the winter anchors itself in ships] of the Bible of nature compose the jewel-boxes the chariots of the Good Child the wedding presents of the Mahadrajah necklace of pink pearls from India (Bechert Bazar) the wedding carriage the wedding flower parade Psyche's jewel-box the palankeens of Spanish Beatrice of Este carried on Easter day in Otero (jewels) of terralita Marie Medicis the museums of idyllic nature paintings. She has her Sedia or portable bed. The she-devil on the balcony of the amphitheater or the temples of Jupiter—or on the sea—Triton in his cloak rolls his golden book of the Creation—under the sun's kisses—as a resplendent Lord of light stretched out the sky like a carpet over his adored feet [in the bed of roses] each page would open into Bonaparte's torn mantle: then dissolves the bouquets or jets of water of flowers of light Bengal lights of Sans Souci all the Siegesallees Colonna around the World Map like a cup of Ship of azure full of multicolored natural monuments. How well you hold this green cup—from the cup Thule sinks into the sea without the Golden oar emanates from golden lanterns Fingalle organs

This imperial crown astral flower of charity blooms in the bed of the imperial car beneath the flowering sceptre of renewal [sumptuous hierophant of seasons stand brazenly on the 7 wonders of the natural world] when the stars write the Lord God by leaning their corollas of fire or their crowns of fire since the chariot of ocean-fire of the Gaurisancar—trailing the nuptial [. . .] veils over Mont-Blanc covers Napoleon [on his Marie-Louise] with tiara stoles where the freedom of America in dancing with the Emperor (so singt und tanzt Amerika in music) all her petticoats that she lifted on nature Freedom in flower sinks in the Leman [Malibran] of azure I saw you blush like lady rosvelt (at Schwilgue as they like it) and with love embellishing you. She crossed Europe a harp attached to her heart she trailed in Her Carriage organs the peoples transported in her arms [of the 7 wonders of the ancient world] Lets stay together like a bouquet of flowers The call of flowers O in the face of adversity let us stay right together like a bouquet of flowers of [magic] light Magnificent togetherness light (of Broadway) and purity it's a ray of flowers (of organs) a cry for help to hearts sanctity sanctity—sacrifice of beauty it's like a song of flowers charity charity

Chrysanthemum—in music little Geisha chrysanthemum in the multiple and changing mirror that crowns with a diadem the Japanese and Chinese people with purple and gold always coiffed for the pleasure of the mikado offering her startled nape outside adorable Kimonos (in O Dove sacrificed on the altar or the flowered banks of Lygia and her Ursus—the wind in the seas blows from Asia on your slashed feathers and bestows an ephemeral royalty to their frenzy. For you brandish over pale winter the flowering sceptre of your disdains And you die in the last love of the garden beauty—by Isabelle Kaiser like saying All the earth blossoms beneath the flowering sceptre of renewal in the robe of love—we clothe the earth in adoring always. God is the name that all adore when the summit turns gold and covers it with a mantle bursting with greenery and life.

The census of Bethlehem and the flight out of Egypt—an angel of the Lord appears in dream to Joseph and tells him to rise take the little child and his mother flee Egypt Matthew 2-13 painting by Fra Angelico.

Quo vadis Domine

Whither goest thou Lord

I saw your beautiful Italian sky bloom and your sirens with veils of Lotus roses on the banks of Lygia crowned in your arms (in the robe of love with which we clothe the royal earth in always adoring God is the name that all adore when the summit [Cimarose] turns gold in its mantle bursting with greenery and life) [on his throne with 7 candalabras 7 wonders of the world] in O dove sacrificed on the altar of Venus de Milo staged theater party had painted as she-devil her mantle of the royal court of the Saviour's diadem her dress of paphos butterflies—of waterlillies—in her bed of roses—to kiss the marble statue dressed as Venus—there remains the monument of Jupiter in the garlands of roses of the psyche threw to her—she throws flowers in his face.

## PROMISES

The vines are flowering and I'm twenty years old Yesterday and in the orchard the apple trees opened only white and pink petals But already today powerful suns have made destiny rejoice Tomorrow the grape will ripen the orchard tomorrow will have apples [Rubens' crown of fruit] Here are fruits flowers leaves and branches in crowns of orange blossoms just fallen in the nuptial bed of roses.

## AUTUMN

A yellow flower whispers The poplars have the shivers One perceives feebly the sound of a cracked and aged bell—From the sky that one can barely see fine drops of drizzle weep and on the black hillock a ruin in silhouette—The evening that watches out for sleepiness spreads its muslin sail The last reflections of the purple setting sun fall behind the hill by J. Rouge

## THE EDELWEISS LEGEND

of Madame Dentan.—As soon as the star had led the three kings to the cradle of the child redeemer—It searched in the cloudless sky—for an azure corner upon which to hang its splendor—Its divine mission ended it needed Nonetheless it was unaware of its sublime destiny . . . where to hide since its brilliant dress (orb) had too quickly eclipsed its rivals . . . it noticed the royal earth immense monstrance and illuminated it . . . it wandered for a long time through mountains and vales without better knowing what humans valued . . . But in seeing Switzerland with its white Alps the fresh valleys where the joyous chalets (Glory to God) wreathed the blue lakes the simple hearted and pious villagers

studied the land as if it were a Christmas tree . . . the star loved
the laughing country and, divided into multiple rays of great
organs by a night of penetrating perfumes, burst forth at the
cimarose of the mountains . . . the next day upon their solar
awakening the herdsmen and the chamois hunters saw the
strange stellar blossoming . . . the white velvet of the ermine
flower star of the kings . . . This is why the edelweiss that always
watches the heavens is happy on the Talisman summits safe to
whoever keeps it . . . good luck charm it never fades as a butterfly
Kursaal dancer the earth sealed to the flower Cleo Merode and
her Julius Caesar—at the little sparrow that gives fodder shall
receive the gifts of nature as a present—in making the eight
crowns of the seasons bloom on Charlemagne's and Corsican
Napoleon's heads—our cook and pope-parson of Rhodes the isle
of roses—Belgian children were pale have become rosy received
bouquets of lotus roses: a human flower of a Mille fleur charity
at the creator Chamorel's the angel Gabriel la Rosiere's cook—
and of all the Hotels of Lausanne Ouchy often free of charge lost
among the stores by thousands . . . Good and Happy new year
each pie a flower Millefleur charity Muller Chamorel being
professor Muller are the Good Children.

TRANSLATED BY SOPHIE HAWKES   (Words in brackets were inserted between the lines by Aloïse Corbaz.)

ALOÏSE CORBAZ   was born in 1886, in Lausanne. She received her
*baccalauréat* in 1906. Though blessed with a beautiful voice, she failed
as a professional singer, and in 1911 she left for Germany and held
positions as a governess and housekeeper at the home of Wilhelm II's
chaplain. The First World War forced her to return to Lausanne. She
then began to express religious, pacifist and humanitarian sentiments
with such zeal that she was committed, in 1918, to the psychiatric
hospital of Cery-sur-Lausanne; and in 1920, and until her death in

1964, to la Rosière à Gimet, an annex to the hospital. Her early work was nearly all destroyed, and it wasn't until 1936 and thereafter that sympathetic doctors became interested in her case, and collected her writings and paintings.

## HENRI MÜLLER

### REPUBLIC THE FREE

Republic The Free Partly Smashed or No Mistake Step The Summoning Somnambulist. It's an absolute hovvel where no one understands a thing and it at times has nothing to do with us, it's a secret and dreaming people they have baroque and diverse ideas they also tell fortunes they are a sort of sorcerer they're big like tall Englishmen all svelte and lean with imaginary ideas. They're not all crazy but pretty nearly it's still a mistake.

O!!! O!!! O. What a mistake, come into my happiness.
O!!! O. Beautiful Republic The Free Partly Smashed.
O!!! O. Beautiful Republic the No Mistake The Summoning Somnambulist be my loves.

They are like that for an idea it's a fashion of their own and they can't help themselves they don't know what they want they are nevertheless just as fine as we are they follow a politics of levelers. It's like those who could be called a top or robot, they have that precision in the soul it's their own idea, they're our sons for sure it's no mistake.

O!!! O!!! O. What a mistake, come into my happiness.
O!!! O!!! O. Beautiful Republic The Free Partly Smashed.

O!!! O. Beautiful Republic the No Mistake The Summoning Somnambulist be my loves.

It's a Beautiful seated Republic their fashions are the sons of their fathers in their souls they have secrets and baroque ideas don't play with them they resort to cold steel. Their war secret is not written they hide it in their spirits it's a new-model precision rifle that no one knows it's a sorcerer's gun of wood, don't be Mistaken.

O!!! O!!! O. What a Mistake, come into my happiness.
O!!! O! Beautiful Republic The No Mistake Summoning Somnambulist be my loves.

It's a new generation with powderless smokeless cold steel noiselessly they march over the earth its their caprice it's a tribute to pay.

---

Song.
The power of Enjoux and Joy and Bomont
From Fairy France all three, Positive, Unitarian, Ephemereal, Arduous, Emancipatory
(Unity is strength)
In the Heavens are three, The Republics and the Unitarian Powers, of Fairy France; (Unity is strength.) And from heady Power Ephemeral of la Gearla, and from an emancipatory Power, juice flowing and sparkling from the stream of joy, and Makers of lemonade, People from Enjoux and Bourgogne and Bomont.

Pumpkin. Lemin. Jokin. Pumpkin. Lemin. Jokin.

God and his lady the Virgin Mary, his priests, the pope and his Saints are all in heaven and in the sky with the Angels and see us at every moment, and could scold us, let's go down into the basement there he won't be able to see us and drink of this sparkling wine of Joy and Enjoux, and beware of the great rooster of Ain and Enjoux hiding at the bottom of the basement and in the rocks of Saut-A-L'ours and Creux de L'Eau.

Pumpkin. Lemin. Jokin. Pumpkin. Lemin. Jokin.

The ladies, they were Queen Berthas of great beauty, they were celestial Divinities, escaped from Heaven to the eternal Father, they were virgins of Plan and Tulip Oak, so they went down to the basement, and saw the room of lemonade casks, and drank without touching their lips to the rim and got drunk and they were forced to take off all their clothes because a farting took place, it was funny, it ran down their legs and they sang their favorite hymn torrents overboard to wake the dead; torrents overboard to wake the dead.

Pumpkin. Lemin. Jokin. Pumpkin. Lemin. Jokin.

and then they danced together men and women pell-mell, and all farting, it was terrible, and it was funny, it was an orgy. The Queens hadn't changed, on the contrary they were more beautiful with their legs all knitted, it was terrible, and it was funny, it was an orgy, it was the Queen Berthas of Heaven, they were divinities of Plan and Tulip Oak, and they danced the waltz of the Roses. O. Tra-la-la. O yes how we drank. O. Tra-la-la. O. Tra-la-la. how we drank.

Pumpkin. Lemin. Jokin. Pumpkin. Lemin. Jokin.

It was the Queen Berthas of heaven, it was the Virgins of the Royal Palace of Enjoux, of Saut-a-L'ours of Joy and Bomont, it was Naked Queens, Queens of heavens, it was the Divinities, and to sing their favorite hymns they climbed up onto the casks, and straddled them, it was a joke, the Misters made the short ladders to the Queens, and they farted and it was funny, and they sang their favorite hymn, pour to the brim this divine juice that wakes the dead, pour to the brim this divine juice that wakes the dead.

Pumpkin. Lemin. Jokin. Pumpkin. Lemin. Jokin.

It was the Queen Berthas of all beauty, it was the stars of Heaven, it was the Virgins, they were completely naked, it was outrageous to see the farts that knitted them all, and their titties hung out, the wine had gladdened them, they had hung their clothes on the sides of the kegs, the lace of the panties and the beautiful white slips dragged in the spilt wine, it was outrageous to see, and they danced the waltz of roses. O. Tra-la-la. O. Tra-la-la. O yes how we drank. O. Tra-la-la. O. Tra-la-la. How we drank.

Pumpkin. Lemin. Jokin. Pumpkin. Lemin. Jokin.

It was the Queen Berthas of all beauty, it was the Divinities of Heaven, it was the Jesus virgins, and then they resorted to a shepherd and his fleece, who fleeced them, because they had farted, it was comical, they were little frogs, it looked like little bells, it was comical how beautiful they were with these little bells, they were Divinities of Heaven. They were Jesus Virgins, and they sang their favorite hymn. Pour to the brim this divine wine, pour to the brim this divine juice.

Pumpkin. Lemin. Jokin. Pumpkin. Lemin. Jokin.

Oh my God, How we drank, and what fun we had, what joy we were all enraged, the Queens' lower bellies were all red and ranks were crossed, it was an orgy, what fun we had, what happiness, what a shame God our husband came to disturb us, what nerve, and they danced the waltz of roses. O. Tra-la-la. O. Tra-la-la. Oh yes how we drank. O. Tra-la-la. O. Tra-la-la. How we drank.

**123**

Pumpkin. Lemin. Jokin. Pumpkin. Lemin. Jokin.

And in the end, it was an indescribable uproar. The Kings of all the Powers came running, to see these Queen Berthas of the Divinity of the Royal Palace of Enjoux, Saut-a-L'ours, Joy and Bomont. And they kissed them and made deep bows to them in spite of the fact that they had farted and were completely naked, they were the Queens of Heaven of the Eternal Father, and they danced all together the Waltz of roses. O. Tra-la-la. O. Tra-la-la. Ah yes, how we drank. O. Tra-la-la. O. Tra-la-la. How we drank.

Pumpkin. Lemin. Jokin. Pumpkin. Lemin. Jokin.


EETERNALL

All come my beauty (come into) my arms come kiss me and
    we'll go
come my Andalusian beauty come let me marry you
and be my beauty my sleeping beauty
come my beauty (come into) my arms come kiss me.
Ah be my beauty . . . whom I summon with a mocking smile
come into my arms come kiss me.
Ah my beauty be the charm and beauty that I love
Ah come into my arms my beauty come kiss me

And be my beauty and the greatness with the mocking smile
the charm and your beauty and spread (over) me our life of
suffering and hope.

Come my beauty into my arms and kiss me
Come my beauty into my arms and kiss me

Ah come my beauty with your smile and your beauty the
secret dream and sure of your affections and our agreements
shall join in an emblem of triumph

the beauty told me that you were from Zorigny and that
you (had the smile of) a Fairy. One might have guessed it . . .

Ti-ti-ti-tru-la-la. The beauty was strange and at nightfall
she cast a mysterious shadow over the grass

---

de ro de
pas la po
De ce me
la et de ro
to fon ce
près ren de
ten le de
men ra de
de ba de cu a ra
du cu de ta ma de pos
de la ra mi no ja pre de te

(de for est
no the po
Of it me
the and de for
a dar ken
near gi ve
in the of
min ther oads
be low de ass a ra
of ass of your my de pos
of the ra me no ja nex to you)

TRANSLATED BY SOPHIE HAWKES

HENRI MÜLLER   Born in 1865 in Boltigen, Switzerland, Müller made a living briefly as a vine grower. Around 1903, he invented a machine with which to trim vines but evidently the idea was stolen from him. This contributed to the onset of mental problems that led him to spend the rest of his days in the Musingen psychiatric hospital in the canton of Berne. There, he built machines that whirled about in total futility, as well as busied himself with drawing. The texts presented here were written on the backs of some of his drawings.


## JULES DOUDIN

Ime thee natcherel iced swizz mye Bax ide woodent gover the whore eye sun. watch choo plain Att Ime sloshing abbot in the mudd. Owe mye arrs yore knot wirth ennything ennything attle. Four the Tomitit. koont flye ova mee Mye Arrs willown lee reap peer wenn Yewve flo nover four the ferry larst ime. Mye ole manse arrs Yewel Sea itter gain bee side the Mount ane Ive hadda nuff bred; Ime get ting owt ter droughn meself. Mye arrs Ile gettit orlback. iff yore nyce tommy. Mye bruthiz cunt tay kit Ive brung mye cell foff timon timon gayne. that swye the prossy cuter reely hazzit infamee

sighned

---

The code Whorizons larst yere
awl thozz Carves Bell ease. The
cold woz in Tents whenn eyewash
in daws the souls of mye pheet
wurr perry shin soak tins punk
Ime awl waze reddy forrers crapp

Varley innis snaz heek are
drop tin att the plaice eye werk
juss thin hizz tigher went flatt
onn the sigh doppo sight mye moosh
ann the whole cloze tite so eye
carnt shit      deer broth her
yore Nay burr senzis best

Jen tall menn Imer batchel ler
Won day mye mouther woz plarnting
      Kabby jess
Wenshee broker legg fromm the topp
hover lad der mye dadspott tedder
hoper ning. Atta corn rov
the streat mye syst her stucca
fing rinnit like ape reast sane grayse
eye shatt mye whole alms foldit
Thenn mye syst her througher
alms surround mye nekk Yore syst
hearse herb itch Getcher sell foam

---

So eyewash holdup at the jollie huzzaz Oppo side the Wight
whorse

Mye purr purse in right ing Ister tellyew a thinger too bean
ayble to staye putt aint summink the lyska yew kandoo Yew eet
lyke piggz. wen Eye git Ohm ittlebee boy lingott Ime loo zing
bludd Inn ear dayday daybyday Ile fiter gains the king derm of
the mowlze. Ive lost tutch with mye selph Ide bee blyged iff yoo
cood spair a pockit hanker cheef for Jools Duddin. who evry
wonn thynx Stynx. Tooby Plucky saye Hang onn Eye cood
Boase toff havvin skraipt throo bye the skinner mye teath. They

diss pize mee they shitten mee. Iff yoo confined any whun nose smudgers mee bough tittall juss sendem upp too seamy inn the king derm Of heavy earn Thattle semmy upper bitt Nuffter grabber thatt littall Dar lingh jest gonn parst. Ime loosing bludd buy the galleon four the saik off a spotter but ter sheen evry ven Hadd Pleez doant briggand mee fur Her

The Governer iz Usher toother juj of payearn

Jules Doudin

---

Ide Unno Iff itz the Rite flour Ive Pict in migh Try Umph. Eye hadda slitt oh pinner butter nole turk atchet; Eye noe howitz Ile rub mye ize ellse Ive bean baddly plaiced inn this Gah dinn Eye diddin phorm the Sea lesty all farther it woz aller foany paye meant witch shooduv bin maid on The hyweigh of the slitt Bellee Sojer from hear abouts Imer hoarse mann in all the pressy peaces they cood fynd no sojer goodaz yoo The wimmin useter leaf verry quite Ime baddly plaiced got propper scaired herring nouthing of mye maitz so Eye pisstoff then gott Back Have alluck if theirs enny walter won of mye eerz herrts badd dont messer bout gimme a hanker chieve ellsyle Screem fore help Migh pokkit adder nole innit sew the butta nopen dupp then inna waive of enthuzzeum the nott dropt all long the royal Weigh at tennin the mourning It woz Perry Shin Coal and mye danda juss droopt

Louise Fauttieh Mye Skool mizz triss Owe shuns sheap sheap mye years pier strong mye poop eel aint lye kew Eye wenter the howse ter sea ware the figher woz Ide herd sum won crigh nowt figher mye alms broak mye lex herd juster buv the ray ling. Eyedash shout inter the feeled too kiddzer cumin outer skool. Doan choo shout noh lowder else aisle lok yupp The woodz cum rite down inter the orch idza long the paive meant My whyffe

yeld owt yew carnt eaven Pyss yoo yew sless bugg her; The Coss
axe fare wont cumbak nome or. the rane forst mee to shutt upp
mye boock. Code wether keyps yer yung pleece send mee as lice
Abredd O That Tahrt sheez prittee ass shooger cannedy. Pleece
justa pounda butta

TRANSLATED BY ROGER CARDINAL

JULES DOUDIN   Jules Doudin was born in the Swiss town of Payerne
in 1884. He was eleven when his alcoholic father hanged himself.
Having worked for a while as a railroad pointsman, Doudin took to
drink after an unhappy love affair. Symptoms of schizophrenia led to
his being interned in 1911 in the Cery clinic near Lausanne, where he
remained until his death in 1946. It was in 1927, long after the onset of
his illness, that he spontaneously pencilled weird caricatures on scrap
paper, producing the bulk of his pictorial work in the space of a few
months.

# FRANCE

## CHRIST INTO THE WATER

DRAWING                    COMPOSITION                    PLATE

Emile Hodinos Josome - Son of Emile Jean Hodinos. Cavalryman of 1848. Lancer of 1859. Infantryman of 1873-1874. Locked
up in Ville Evrard for no good reason. For twenty full years: from
December 15, 1876 to the month of     . Moulder - Modeller -
Inventor - Typesetter - Compositor - miniaturizer - Engraver of
Medallions - Infantryman 2nd cl. Volunteered for one year
under the 1872 scheme. Paid 1500 francs as Volunteer in the 1st
Batallion of the 5th Company of the Line at the Oratory Barracks. Matriculatin number 11072. Is–re - Grenoble - Province -
of the Dauphinee - size - or rather Height 1 m. 75 centimetres.
Forehead medium - Hair Black - Dark Brown. Beard same or
clean shaven. Eyes medium - Nose aquiline - mouth medium.
Cheekbones prominent - Distinctive Features: two scars on For-
head. Eyebrows, eyelashes, moustache. Chin round - Musket
drill - Marches - Sharpshooter's training - Bayonet drill - One
tunic - One jacket - One pair red trousers - One pair militia
trousers - One cape. Two pairs hobnail boots. One black canvas
kitbag - Set of Brushes - Button-stick - Sewing kit - Composed of
one Pair of Scissors, one Thimble, One Cotton reel - Marking
thread. Black and White thread. Some Buttons - Two Shirts -
One Pair of Sheets - One Palliass - One Mattress - One pillow -
One blanket - Two bolsters - Three planks - one Mess-tin - One
Spoon - One two pound Loaf - Drills of the Esplanade - the
Polygon - Sleeves - Camps - Pegs - Canvas tent - Rope - Straps.
Once into the water. Sort of ramparts outside Town - Once into
the Water at the Cours la Reine pool. Once into the Water in the
ponds of the Municipal Gardens. Into the Water on the Rue des
Quatre vents, into the Water on Place St Sulpice In the course of

the years 1875-1876 Evrard - Baths - Showers - Straightjackets - Several Baths During the years 1877-1878-1880-1881-1882-1883-1884-85-86-87-88-89-90. During the years 1891, 1892, Bathing suspended. Bathing regularly each week. During the years 1893-1894-1895-1896-1897 approximately - Fed - watered - clothed at the Ville Evrard. Make my bed quite regularly. Empty out my Chamber Pot. Drawing - Writing - The - Brushing my shoes - Cleaning my Combs - Hair fallen out - Courtyard of Pavilion No 3. Drawing Throughout the Years 86, 87, 88, 89, 90, 91, 92, 93, 94, 95, 96, 97.


SLAVONIC PASSION

All day. Next morning - mutual friend - relative - Count - Monte Carlo - track down - tall order - sitting - hours - terrace - café - Hotel - Paris - reading - Newspapers - appearance - reality - observing - passers-by - strolling - palm trees - entered - Casino - time - get up - circulate - Gaming - hall - meet - Parisians - believe - Africa - Astonishment - seeing - everyone - assuming - intimate - attitudes - take leave - words - Now then - Young - man - decidedly - there's - celebrity - those absent - in the wrong - Trouble - getting rid - intruders - Nobody - Could - oblige - waited - retained - elsewhere - ask - explicitly - let - slip - chance - name - Russian - general - one remarked - dead- nihilists - assassinated - last year - other shrieked - dined - winter - ambassador - Petersburg - chestnut - whiskers - ferocious - air - rolls - eyes - proper - Cossack - Pretends - Europe - world - Acquainted - dinner - establishment of class - English café - must have set - Feet - boulevard - Evening - drawing in - desperation - character - feel - inflamed - desire - fortify - determination - approached - girl - ah well - would anywhere else - example - Should follow - return - home - without seeing again - house - left - many -

months - previously - difficulty - vanquish - opposition - destiny
- thwart - Implement - energies - be established - struggle - Some
people - think - when they chat - that one - lived - tooth and nail
- confronting - resistance - obstacle - Gaming - hall - ten o'clock
- circulated - tables - suddenly - saw - right - before - him - thirty
- forty - wide shoulders - Russian - sitting - at - green - baize -
playing - enormous - stakes - three - rounds - rake - removed -
five - six - thousand - francs - turn around - held out - hand -
someone - behind him - hand - Deposit - bundle - Bank - notes -
Want - lifted up - arm - held out - bundle - Count - arm -
corpulent - long - sleeve - green - cloth - red - fringes - gold
buttons - belonged - colossal - footman - wearing - strange -
livery - tall - man - master - face - half extinguished - framed -
chestnut beard - bushy - hair - color - eyebrows - thickets - Small
eyes - brutal - expression - insistent - piercing - rotating - slowly -
all - directions - returning - point - came from - then off again -
in front - to the side - to right - to left - imperceptible pause -
each object - each face - seeking what - lowered - had noticed -
time - hand - opened - still - Count - selected - bank - notes -
wallet - powerful - fingers - closing - catch - fastened - finished -
examining - person - five - fingers - raised - opened - clasp - took
- new - packet - notes - passed - Count - Devil - thought - young
- man - gesture - executed - single hand - left hand - dying - to
know - right arm - disabled - occupied - Marquis - moved -
behind - moutchik - all smiles - pleated - livery - waist -
underskirt - Russian - peasant - loose - hand - huge cane - dark
wood - silver knob - Does - cane - Count - Does - arm - demands
- Marquis - servant - perhaps - lifeguard - condemned - secret -
committees - Around them - hardly - paid - attention - wild -
face - bizarre - costume - the man - wallet - gambling - absorbed
- audience - Furthermore - multicolored - interior - sees -
astonishment - all - masquerades - the yuniverse - pasing by -
Hand - touched - shoulder - Marquis - voice - murmured - look -

too much - lovely eyes - uneasy - observe - skeletons - danse macabre - just - sat down - place - croupier - not caused - stupefaction - turned about - prepared - take offense - Sir - But - immediately - he smiled - held out - hand - what now - dear friend - it is you - Before - was - man - forty - forty-five - years - on the whole - medium height - weakish - face - grey eyes - extreme - delicacy - not much - sparkle - eyeglasses - moustache - still black - skilfully dyed - intelligent forehead - bared - beneath - frizzy - thinning - lovely hair - silvery - discreetly - tinted - pale - tiny - laugh-lines - Parisian night-owl - greeted - foreign - name - he continued - shaking - hands - afresh - this is - meeting - But - must - begin - thank - you - seems that - you - have - achieved - extraordinary - feat - was - journalists - best-placed - world - to - transmit - anything - required - Paris correspondent - London - Herald - had - disposal - or - all - indispensable - means -

Cat - woman - mantelpiece - Mirror - Bedroom - Frame - Bust, woman, Frame - woman's head in Profile, hair, cape, frame - Bust, girl , foot turned out, Plinth, frame - Head in the round, woman, posing on pedestal, frame - decoration with 5 branches Oakleaf or laurel crown surround, republican head at midpoint, crown or flags as hinge, collar, frame - Bust of girl, square base, frame - Head in the round, man, posing on a pedestal, frame - full-length figure of a woman standing on a Plinth, draped, frame - Torso of a young man, below his head in Profil, turning to Left, with Left hand on abdomen, right hand hanging down perpendicularly, right forearm, posed upright, almost perpendicular, frame - Girl, full length a head at Left, in the background, male head in Profile, draped figure - female figure, full length, holding a corset in left hand, Satin Bodice, white Petticoat, the words white Petticoat, Satin Bodice in Italic Lettering, frame - A packet of medallions - Bodice, medal, the word Bodice in capital letters, woman, head in Profile, turning to right, her right hand open, held away from the body to her right, arm and forearm, also the left hand Held down slightly away from the body to her left side. The left Nee placed on the Plinth. The Left Foot flat to the ground. The right thigh, placed horizontally, the Right Foot posed horizontally in Profile, bears Down upon the Plinth, frame - Thick. White Nanzook Petticoat. - Medallion of 0.040 millimetres in diameter, the words, Thick. White Nanzook Petticoat, in capital letters. The center is taken up by a female figure, one nee on the ground. The right Foot seen Frontally placed vertically on the Plinth. The right hand open. The arm and forearm as well as the Left hand hanging down beside the body and the thigh, Frame - Female figure upright with weight on right Foot seen in Profile, The Left Foot seen in three-quarter view, The nees tensed but not locked, the body upright on its hips, the shoulders Held horizontally, the head three-quarter view, turned to the left. The left hand raised, the right hand Hanging down. Shirt, Belt, navel, a drape Falling to the right of the figure and over the Plinth. A Frame - Bust of Girl, upon a square Base, frame - the name E. HODINOS J. in capital letters, Set within a rectangle, a Small rectangle at bottom, all but square - A seated female figure, her head leaning, three-quarter view, inclined to the Left, Her Left hand raised as well as the arm and forearm. The right arm hanging vertically, the elbow Bent, the right forearm Posed obliquely, the right hand viewed from behind almost horizontal, including the fingers. A long neck, Prominent breasts. Perpendicular Torso, pelvis at an angle, seated figure, Bodice, Thighs inclined to the right. The nees in three-quarter view. The right leg Placed all but Perpendicularly, the right Foot, in Profile, set upon the Plinth - The Left Leg vertically inclined. The Left Foot lifted and Set down flat upon the Plinth. A petticoat. This figure draped in a Mantle, the whole framed -

The Romans and the Greeks, were masters at producing squares, rectangles, circumferences, letters, edgings of Pearls, listels, inscriptions, they well knew that corners could be turned, dipped, unstuck, modelled, drawn, composed, the crown of oakleaves and the crown of laurel and oak with their branches and their Tiny ribbons. They knew how to fashion Medallions in pewter, in zinc, in moulds, in Plaster, in bronze in silver in gold. These were made as rewards for Warriors, male and female, artisans, astronomers, farmers, industrialists, shopkeepers, apprentices, and all classes of society. In memory of or to commemorate the founding of Monuments, Public buildings, Bridges, roads, Promenades, Sewers, Pavements, Boulevards, Streets, Squares, Gardens, arboriculture Horticulture. Stock-farming. Railways. Vehicles, lorries, etc., they were called commemorative Medallions, in memory of the founding of Cities, of a captain who had won a battle, the establishement of a fortress - The Capturing of a Piece of cannon from the Enemy, a fortification. Law Courts, a Church. A temple, a triumphal Arch. The Planting of a wood. In Rome the Romans Spent their time Modelling Drawing, inventing ways to Miniaturize and also to Engrave Medallions; and so it was with the Greeks, who represented, on their Medallions all the cities of Greece, crowns, escutcheons, fleur-de-lis, the names of Engravers.

Both the Romans and the Greeks engraved on steel.
Rome had the Mint - Romulus
Greece had its Own one too - Athens
And then all the other Nations of the Entire World.

---

Emile Hodinos Josome. Constable. Volunteer one year. Communard. Cavalryman of 1848. Emile Jean Charles Hodinos, his father. Commander-in-chief of the armies of the Republic.

Baker. Self-employed - three shops, at his death left to his son
E. Josome Hodinos the sum of 25,000 francs accruing or deriv-
ing from the sale of his Baker's business. One shop on Rue St
Martin No 115. The other on Rue Madame. The other Avenue
de Breteuil. Left Boarding school at 16, where he had been a
boarder for four years, one day as Day-boy - Apprenticed with
Tasset, Master Engraver of Medallions. Took classes in Engraving for 4 years, from half pass Twelve, one o'clock to 7 in the
Evening in winter, from Twelve to half pass Twelve one o'clock
to 6 in summer. Incised squares, rectangles, escutcheons, fleur-
de-lis, heraldic eagles, Bands, crowns, heraldic horses Lions,
Oakleaves, laurel leaves, oak crowns, laurel crowns, ribbons -
moulded in wax on slate, a bee, an escutcheon with its garter, a
tiny saint's medallion: constructed moulds, watched how to
miniaturize, to cast iron, to mould models, watched how to
mould wax, to draw arms hands, to make a bust, medallions.
Commerce, Industry, Navigation, the Pope, a saint's medallion.
Sets of Coins. Republic of Honduras. Crowns of Oakleaves, of
Laurels. Parmenter known as the Potato Man, Medallions to the
right and to the left. Watched how to incise, to mill, to soak, to
rotate, to heat up. Balls, pads, gouges, the oil Stone, Sheep's Foot
oil. Magnifying lens, Vice, hammers, weights, templates, files,
the saddle, the 2 manikins, the Plasters, the lamp turned up.
The holders crammed with letters. Watched how to make a bust,
to scale down, to sharpen up the Gouges. Industry - The Ro-
bineau Works. The Vieuxmaire Works. The Herne Works. The
Agry Works. The Esparon Works. The Frotain Works. The
Hirche Works. The Visiting Card Works. The works for stamping
and embossing. The works for diplomas. The Bagriot Works. The
Lonchaye Works and two or three others. The Mint.

Sent to the School of Drawing on Rue de l'Ecole de
Médecine, he drew and made models, for 2 years from 8.30 to
12.30 and from 7 to 9 in the Evening.

Then did one year's Voluntary service in the 52nd from November 1873 to Novemeber 1874. Paid the 1500 fr. as volunteer, joined the 1st Battalion 5th Company, Barracks of the Isére Oratory - Grenoble Province of the Dauphiné Number 1072 attended Military School. Marching drills, sharpshooting, bayonet drill. Battalion school, parade ground service, field service. Guard Duty at the Oratory barracks, at the archbishop's palace, behind or on the Left side of Barracks. On the Place de la Division. At the Porte des Alpes. On Manoeuvres. Forced marches. Target practice. Military parades. Reviews at the Esplanade and the Polygon.

Two years in Art School, made models, drawings, compositions, moulds.

Locked up in the Ville Evrard on 15 December 1876.

Has kept entries in the visitor's book, and both Laundry books. His Medallions, drawn in pencil, gone over in Ink, composed, right down to the surrounds, the fillets of Pearls. Embossed Borders. Drapes. Women. Old men. Men and children. Notables of the Republic. Undertitles. They Bear - Muscles and Osteology - Glossary of Undertitles. Counted out the bed linen, set out the bed linen, made his bed, emptied his Chamber pot, brushed his breeches, changed the bed linen, changed his clothes and his shoes. Ate, slept, drank, went to the latrines. Brushed his shoes, watered, looked after the. . . , fetched the soup, went for a walk, lay down on the grass. Took a train, shook out his curtains. (Is composing his Biography. Writings as a Boarder. Dictation. Stories. Grammatical Analysis. Logical Analysis. Natural History. Geography - Physics - Chemistry - Accounting - Arithmetic - Geometry - History - Grammar the Ten Parts of Speech - Surveying - Describes his workshop - Describes his incarceration at the Ville Evrard.

Emile Hodinos Josome. Is of medium height. The size of his head equals the distance from the underside of his chin to the

lower limit of his Pectorals, from his Pectorals to his navel, from
his navel to the line of his belly, his shoulders measure two heads
long, his expanded Chest makes his ribs stand out, and the end
of the Sertorum - the clavicles, the humerus, the pelvis, the joints
of the femur, the Cubitus and the radius. The frontal, a section of
the Parietal, the temporals. The rim of the eyesockets. The eye-
balls. His hair, his beard, his moustache, his aquiline nose, his
medium-size mouth, his round chin his cheekbones. The upper
lip and the lower lip, the nose, the nostrils, his look his eyes, his
Eyelids. It is rounded on the upper Part (convex) rounded on the
Right part (convex) rounded on the lower part (convex) rounded
on the Left Part (convex) a perpendicular line forms the neck on
the left-hand side, the left ear can be seen, his parting is to the
left (hair). The collar of the jacket, tunic, cut low beneath the
throat, a tie the army one his decoration. The first button of his
tunic done up, a pair of Epaulettes on his shoulders (red). Yellow
collar. Buttons of brass (polished). A shirt his army one a red or
blue belt (tie) doing service as a belt. His red Trousers, his
uniform Tucks and shapes itself perfectly around the waist on
either side, his coattails fall nicely, his arms hang naturally, his
head in three quarter view turned to the right; Six buttonholes
and six buttons on his greatcoat (tunic). His convex Shoulders
rounded on the outside on top. His convex arms rounded on the
outside on the right and left sides; Convex on the inside on the
sides of the two arms, convex Sections of the left and right hand
sides. Tunic undone to show the shirt belt and trousers. 7 Pleats
in his tunic on the right side; 6 pleats on the left side. this is how
the man looks. Pleats at his belt, at the Level of his privates
where bulges above the testicles. the body held upright on its
hips, the abdominals are in place as are the navel, the Pectorals.
The clavicles. Shoulders drawn back, arms held naturally beside
the body as are the forearms, a button can be made out on his
shirt. Decorated with five branches, (oakleaves, laurel leaves)

attached to flags or clustered arms. Head of the Republic, his Own.

Two horizontal lines along top, the word Medallions written in capital or cursive letters; two horizontal lines underneath: the words E. Hodinos J. in capital or cursive letters at midpoint. Two Perpendiculars at the extremities. A Perpendicular occupying the center or the midpoint. The whole thing forms a rectangle. Two tangenital circumferences; for the diameter of my medallions. To find the center of my circumferences. I took the middle of the Perpendicular lines which gave me points, I drew a horizontal line through these points. Next I marked this horizontal line at two other points where the midpoint of the squares, I traced the Perpendiculars through, I found the center of my circumferences. From the midpoint I described two circumferences, touching the four points of my squares. Next I inscribed below in italic characters; the words: moulder, modeller, inventor, compositor, draughtsman, miniaturizer, Engraver of Medallions: Inscribed above also in italic characters, the words: Drawing, composition, Plate. The inscription underneath is set out on my Medallions in the following fashion: tracing out two similar curved lines equidistant; distance apart corresponding to the height of the letters, which are in capital or cursive lettering, taking care that the two sides in balance, the letters being of the same height as width, equidistant from one another. The figure set out with its Proportions, its design, its drapes, its protuberances, its Planes, its Folds, the head in its proper Place, the hair, the eyes, the nose, the mouth, the chin, the Cheekbones, the ears. The eyebrows, the eyelashes, the eyelids, the upper lip, the lower lip, the neck, the Pectorals, the breasts. The arms, the forearms, the hands, the torso, the line of the pelvis, the pelvis, the ribs, the thighs, the nee-caps, the legs, the Feet and the Toes. For surround an embossed edging, a fillet of Pearls, a Plinth, the two

Feet set upon the Plinth. The figure anatomanized. Osteological section. Anatomical section. (. . . .)

In my 10 volumes of medallions put together to demonstrate what a true medallion should be, I have spent eleven year on this. I divided sheets of biscuit paper vertically in two then horizontally in two which gave me 4 small sheets each time. Next I cut out 200 others in 4 equal parts, which gave me 400 sheets. On these 400 sheets, I drew my rectangles, my medallions in pencil which gave me $400 \times 4 = 1600$ pencil medallions, gone over in ink $1600 + 1600 = 3200$ medallions in ink and pencil, figure designs composed drawn in ink and pencil.

Materials used, Paper, pencils, Pens, Penholders, ink, knife, erasers, strips of Paper to check dimensions failing use of compass or dividers, stitched exercise books, lined sheets of Paper.

INSCRIPTIONS: Fine stable, horse, carriage, large bedroom, ship, bachelor apartment, comfortable furnished apartment, drawing room, dining room, divan-bed, private house. Convenient - ground floor, independent access - delightful mezzanine - Quiet person, Large shop, basement - living area at rear - Fine town house - Study
Ville-Evrard 16th May 1896

Emile Hodinos Josome

TRANSLATED BY ROGER CARDINAL

EMILE JOSOME HODINOS "moulder - modeller - inventor - compositor - Draughtsman - miniaturizer - Engraver" Joseph Ménétrier, an engraver's apprentice, was born in Paris in 1853, and was interned at the age of 23 in the Ville-Evrard asylum, remaining there, it is believed, until his death around the turn of the century. Adopting the grandiose pseudonym Emile Josome Hodinos, he devoted all his energies to sketching, writing and composing.

are there still any Judges left in France

I've just been to court been in a court of Justice to listen to the proceeding

a Judge? indeed didn't want to deliver the Death penalty on the accused so I can hear people saying all round me that's disgusting that's disgusting and repeating it one after the Other turn and turn abut the people whatsmore you can't believe 1 word of the evidence they give. our courts of Justice are packed with touts lawyers without clients - the persin the person who takes no pride in his team whatsmore teetotaller on his mother's side Frederine Learolland the daughter of Banville the grandaughter of a grocer Haberdasher ran a cafe cigarettes liqueurs where they sold clothes fashions shoes boots never touched a drop nor did he ever smoke saw all the drawbacks far from it me Moret sur loing Montigny Mazarines Levasseur suresnes aunteebs he's the one sees and hears great eyesight great hearing tells you what he sees and what he hears it's well-known everyone keeps an eye on how he speaks so they keep their Grammar up to scratch Gramma Jayet. . .


## QUIZ

What is the largest of the carnivores?
What is the largest of the carnivoresses?
What is a quincipal? Boissel
What is a quincipress? Bridet
where were you born? on place carpeaux
anglish clay?
Slush of stone?
Vengeance for Albert

Bussy the younger?
what does de Bussy mean? god's skin
what does I've had my furglow mean?
what does I've had my furlough mean?
wenwun is tough a tough lady should one get married?
ought not the wife to follow her husband?
Which is the stronger of 2 spouses?
Who is the one who holds the Flanges on a plough
What does the old mother do meanwhile?
Who does a good job cooking meals?
Who is it gathers in the apples?
Who is it makes great cider?
Who is it makes great tipple?
Who is it makes a great brandy?
What is that great pip that gives off gas?
where do you get the animals from?
horns claws skins earth oceans?
what is the man who produces on earth Sea?
What is the woman who produces on earth Sea?
What is the man who lights up the daylights?
What is the woman who lights up the great Nights?
What merit has the man who devours?
What meritess the woman who devours?
Why should a lad not get married?
At what age should a lad get married?
What are military commitments?
At what age can a girl get engaged?
To whom should her heart be opened?
Is it the father the mother?
should a girl follow her suitor?
far from her parents' watchful eye?
wyefur are lovers desseetful?
who is it brings temptation?

Goodevil when the Parents aren't around?
tiny huge Uvvingweed?
where is the camp of châlons?
where is the camp of cormeilles?
where is the camp of satory?
where is the potter red potter?
where is the potter white and blue?
where is the camp of Mailly?
where is the camp of sissonne?
where is the camp of verdun?
where is the camp of lunéville?
What is the Montfaucon?
What is an arsenal?
who wants arsenal of saltpeter?
What is meant by the word Fortress?
What is the meaning of the word forticate?
Why do we set sail on the high seas?
where does the english channel actually start?
Where did it get its name from?
Why can't a Ram swim for very long?
why can't a ewe swim even less long?
would a mare swim less long than a stallion?
would a bull swim less long than a cow?
would a nanny swim less long than a billy?
What's the point of this difference?
would a man swim longer than his wife?
little kids girls boys watch out?
you all need days and nights before you go leaping over brooks
streams rivers Seas oceans
Why do we sing I must away
And see my Normandy once more?
that is the country I was born?

where does Normandy actually start?
What is meant by a cliff?
where was William the Conqueror born?
where was queen Mathilda born?
where is dives? deauville?
where is cabourg? trouville?
where is Bavent? dozulé?
what makes us start singing?
wenwee step on the cow planks?
1 Which is more intelligent the dresser
4 or the one who needs his wound dressed?
5 What is a packet of bandages?
6 what meritess has a Mother who watches over children?
7 why does a lad run after 36 girls?
8 why does a girl run after the lads?
9 what might happen if this is the case?
10 what's meant by look out the randy lads?
11 what's meant by look out the randy girls?
12 what is meant by the word affair?
13 Why is it a young girl ought not to?
14 Have an affair before she gets Married?
15 should it be the same for the young Man?
16 reply to the parents who censor letters?
17 what is meant by the word insects?
18 what is meant by the word Bacilli?
19 what is meant by the word germs?
20 what is meant by the word Ladie?
21 what is meant by the word jadies?
22 what is meant by the Word Arcray?
23 what is meant by the word Marly le Roy?
24 what is meant by the word Kingdom?
25 where is the very first China Shop?

26 White pots Red pots
27 where is the governor of the prison?
28 What is his name? neither tipple nor trout

## PAGE 13 RIVETTE

Dere holly Further
ime just Tuesdup with it awl you know I wont standard dogs
lambs fleaze pussies lice the Berbons I wont standard you know
perfect leewell I wont tangle with polly ticks gobbleup Lie
gadflies on parade the good soda millet airy march parts leave
that bee I can cope so much the worse for Margaret grizzly lists
electors elactors-actress Dye ink from Bronchitis Bronkeye twice
my heart inundated in good faith my chosen prophets Mahomet
under ground the Breton Sailer little wan the ghoul closes its
eyes to natter closes its gob at every paws so those animals
opening their cowl are forced to shut up those birdles those worn
out poisons get really thirsty joker Scoff pug right youthicky
canter Burr Hive Guzzled all the hooch getcha hands off theirs
bags of fine stuff brandy sider drink up his english clay liquor
makes you tighter than the desert sands. . .

---

beneath the tiny
virgin Rouen its blood
pure as pearl its blood
pure as brine convince
the convinced italian
trumen with surplices
at their bellies grey saint
with child saint near

tank tresses crowns
Marcel Morin Morgues
Modest testers Hermitage
overpowed overshelmed
lessons in mora litty
att Markit vegetables
seeds fodder
granaries cleaned out

---

Halleluiah within Your nest we'll plant a pritty littel gold finch golden sheaves longstreet will make immolayshun bitter folk watch circuits water from my appall bran dee up my sleeve coz victory for my native land is limit loss for the tollgates two chaspels Puppets are so tiny inri has dominions lets take holdwith one step on the meadow if teeth corvetto market Bordello curoweight with novelty pancakes Pana my Mama dyers street villa for life by the banks of the river ore below the fishmarkets antwerp is the fishpond gotha cup the ones condamined damn your spozed to offer your pussy before Mezzidon nor jackalvary saint Mary anne wont be offended sais sarah Bernard congrats in the days report Bar eustache the Market charon washed Maria Birague not antoine Barbey Jouy at Josas Hotel Charlemagne arights odd

TRANSLATED BY ROGER CARDINAL

AIMABLE JAYET Born in 1883, Aimable Jayet came from a poor farming background in Normandy. He was twice married, saw service in the Great War, and set up shop as a butcher. In later life he became mentally unstable, and a suicide attempt led to his internment at the age of 51; he was to spend the rest of his life in institutional care. The texts presented here all date from 1949; it is assumed that Jayet died shortly thereafter.

# SYLVAIN LECOCQ

7 Saint Jean de Dieu the Commander
25th Haily 1949. Retro pest if

Ah! that glass of white wine one quaffs under neath the barrel
when the girls are truly dazzlers on our own people's side; and
then from time to time to the air of some ancient rome ance in
the style and rhy thm in the meddows in the meadows on our
own on our own people's side. Heil Hitler. heil eil ile el L. Who
was it made those little corporals sprout wings Napoleon Hitler?
God by papal decree and the 3rd dit toe. A whole slogan of
reflexions are raised. Sin ce we are aware that all the events
which took place up until that time were transmitted and con-
sumed in preparation for the world wide development, let us
address their principal numbers which have made them into
absolutes by way of cycles readjustable to the very elements of
sequences. To impose one's way upon the human masses it is
necessary first to poscess talents capable of serving such masses.
Now we all have talents more or less but we have to recognize
that those two had universal talents which were recognized
thanks to their initiative and above all the success of their
enterprises. Driven by impulses (God) directed by the papal
guidance (God) but at the mercy of temptation (devil) We all
know temptation in the guise of various forms of get rich quick
whose principles are the public trusts that is material powers
which are insatiable for the deep powers of pride gob and bum.
Eve you are still amongst us. You slag. Why you've really
exploited those who get excited once they spot your lovely eyes
and all you have to do is squeeze them to the caprice of your
senses. Woman you've made mankind a martyr. You've forced
men to kill one another to poscess you to the point of submitting
to blows, not to mention the seed they've sown within you

innocent childhood. You've made Lion or sheep out of those mighty bulls the generators of races. You wanted to become the undisputed mistress through sheer force of your allure from God directed in diabolical ways Hey that corsica's a woman my dear friends. She's the one should implore a caress which adds so much pleasure to the act of copulation You must be strong and never give in unwittingly only after a wise and well calculated reflection. You must no longer allow yourselves to be seen as slaves to love. Only thus will you set the world back on its feet by destroying the notion of the devil and his temptations. You'd always have lost the fight if you'd proceeded any differently for as you all must know it is easier to keep your mouth open than your arm outstretched. The container empties out and gets refilled with a simple effort but the liquid has to be fetched from source. The latter is near at hand the former is often a long long way off.

Sylvain Lecocq

Try to guess at the splotches went into a color drawing.


3 Saint Jean de Dieu workaday
20th Hail y 1949

The international oh oh oh Its eemzit snoon theyre all asinging and alarfing, boo kayze of flough whirrs triffick flatter ease Sweeten love ink Kiskis hartspur ledged 4 a hole Day. Allsorts of dee zires, allsorts of dee lights. My hearty scray zee bee a sweetie take you phing erzoff angel ann dee mon Im dell irius Im alyours. Come here repligh hay try this 1 jewery member that creep told you Dolor oza sheez the womb ann of suffering Do lor oza her kisses bring such bad luck Just watch out if you give her your heart, from that day yule cursor thin tyre hume ann race. Eechfureech and Awfurawl A slight correction must be emphasized so that everybody may verify the metaphysics of life throughout all its manifestations. To this end let us take up the box of cull lures which Doctor Bernard donated to me once he realized I could defend myself (an expression used in many disciplines). 13 colors are comprised. Beyond these you mustn't overlook the range accessible through mixing. Thus the white becomes the dominant hue and dispels every last quibble. We may say in passing that it is no different with the white race which is the most refined. The example afforded by colors is basis of material existence. This mixture of hues is not unlike the mixture of metals where proportion is the key. Now that we have grasped all the factors which make our world rotate backwards by an overload of proportions we shall stick to the basics of the purest hues and, by way of gradual regressions we shall bring them up to the peak of perfection, for continual mingling will only affect grey. So as to attain the rascial proportions such as we envisage them natural laws must immediately enter to effect whereby associations can only be tolerated between similar hues It is our desire though we all be brothers to preserve the purity of rascial distinction which we will come to appreciate every one of us in each case its specific beauty. The great mixtures of blood produce frantic agitation to acclimatize everything in one. Such is life in our times a life full of crises brought about by limited understanding. The medley of colors given above should open up your memory to the need to unify the dominant races beneath a single flag the flag of the international.

Escent shall               S. Lecocq                    prince apple

---

24/9/49. Cant stand sting noble (Constantinople) Turkey you can have back your capital, its name is no longer part of the risk. Hero she ma (ma = my action) Nag a sarky? Philly pines Bee key? knee Hell ego land (They wiped it out) Pa rice knew, york (Ham) Rum Lundonn Genever Burlynn Mad rhydd. Vee enna, Singer paw, Moss cow, Brustles, Ham stir damn, Stock home, (Sam harry ten (Say marty hen) Sir marry ten). Hymn allay her Corps dill error. Your alls? Monty Blanks! Just see how good I am at chess! Your rook watch out you've lost you've lead meat ache it. Queen's pawn bishop it's the night deef ending the King. Metal wire or cheesewire Simples eye mon Mr Punch Charles the Fifth and Luther Chris toffer column bus Ear temple knees. Cranium shoulder arm. Fingers foot stomach brain nose mouth! Cows basin sheep. Hens Roosters chicker dee nilly-nilly. Kasablanca Boulogne Paris Cigar. Dirigible balloon khyte. Arnonicomoflaming. Kimonilastic. Seedy bra hymn. Car dove tailing Congoo. Nylon wool Coton. Wheat oats dandylion. Sundy Corly. Halfweigh halfweigh Peezolour Tutch tastic. Ligrament conitent. Clergy Cardinal Popey pip. Chynese, French Germane Amerrycan England. Red lipstick great stuff. Antartic adriatic Atlantic. Mediterranean. Affrica Pacific Black cattaclysm allah bubble. Fog drizzle Spring Blue sky Dawn Pencil X 1000-2. Unsway one n two. Ob hay 100 hun dread. Cigarette. stub ash envelope ing. Cindrella old Ma Twankey. Rightup the Evil whole. Shah spipe hubble bub Bounced cheque. Go Ann. Toss ex equo Frigates Tawny Owl kestrel Magpie. Rook. Ducks nightingales blackbirds warblers. Cold Frozen sweetmeats melting March April May June July August centuries Creator. Messagie Worldwhy Wart trees waves. Titolike snuff. Whitadonna lil coco 1 White Durious Ball once who veneer. 24/9/49. Zlong theirs yours tars neath the vorts of heaven theirl be Happy nessin the faithless night Seams that scald Sylvareen Sig her etts. Elect roe mahogony tick science bimbam. Their thou sand a year star ting midge oon. Nigh nut tea nun dread and fifth tee. Butterfly whose wings bring us fine weather you know the latest about the new defusing juice. It had to be specially mixed to include all the necessary instinks it's made to measure like his godfather. It's not just children of kings get given fabulous presents when they're born.

Yes it was a Sunday morning Sleepless.            S. Lecocq

Saint Jean de Dieu 28th No vember 1948.

Two fingers up your nose you can always pull 'em out. Once you make allowance for each thing the moater nicely managed will give topper formants. Then you've every right to show your mates whose in the dry ving cete. The finshing line has always been the career goal of the tortoise with its devil the hair. To equalize this would'nt mean shewing up the earth no more than taking some really ancient hillock to build stone on stown in that good old hydraulic quicklime clinker style. Sea stone never was much good for building. It retains salt in its pores which means it gives out humidity once the temperature is damp. Marble has to be carefully monitored when its extraction. It's been kept up by phony competition sew it's up to us its fine sparkling contours. Such loveliness won't you enhance young new world, so many fantastic monumounds built for sheer joy to bold designs linked to the latest techniques and secular stipula-rounds. Sow shall we begin by suppressing all those historic classifounds which only yield washed-up results. What we need is novelty beauty a style for every seasons and from every corner of the globe. Let us show the fraternity of artistic effects in the selfsame way we're to be united Let us unite our heart it's Chrism hers, it's mine, it's ours. Not the 25th but the 30th last December. Researcher is more scientific he's creative. Let us pay homage to the science of sciences which established the month its day zero and its birth 3.flee Why not bid welcome to the redeemer of the world through the feast of wondrous love restored now and for all

time? Let's go to it and not hold back. Yet the table tips up for the
sign of the naked cross then for the gigolo at eight o'clock midnight it's the time for crime. Stay put in the warm and stuff the
good god diffused in your belly down the 1st gullet of the 2nd gull
ate thigh. Songs and music why you've enough notes to make the
whole earth vibrate. You say you'll not invite me? Maybe I'll turn
up the perfect guest if theirs only twelve I don't mind being the
thirteenth. For once at Christ Mass he'd be prescent at the gathering and seeing it's him who'd be honored he'd try his best to put
away the pud dinghy. It won't go down not after all that dry bread
he's scoffed. I think of you when I weigh cup and from a phar my
eyes flow you. I sea you one smore when I sleep in dreams fuller
Miss Tree. I swear to you in my burning pash shone to tell you one
smore I love you grov lingon mine ease there it is this is what I
wanted to tell you but a lass I'm too scared of the loonies. (Ali and
my cone) I've wept so much for you suffered so much to soften
your heart cruel one, I have spent so many days so many nights
thinking of you alone. Sad fate which always prompts such floods
of tears, yet I surrender all my tears at the entrance to your hearts.
Yes I was whicket but can you begrudge me not when I re turn to
beg your for give ness. Ah woman you were crazy didn't you real
eyes one day, you'd have to pay back in love, your hole randsome
of mizz airy.

S. Lecocq

Saint Jean de Dieu 24th August 1949

Pee hero leaving the cab array after a hell over weak: He'd drunk
a light wine and was singing in the drank quill night. Goo deven
ing mad damn moon goo deven ing; goody venning madam oon
goody venning. it's your old pal Pee hero whose come to sea you;
gould Every ning ma dammer Mooner. Pierrot's a bit of a drunk

whose allways whys cracking coz he's got a bottler brand dee and is shore to have done it proud. Deduce therefrom the perfect science of the scalpel. Scalpalaugh, scalpagiggle. Whether it be in your songs, your words, your writings, any of those things you displace in your work, your loves, your sufferings, none of it is other than a pretext for them to indulge in zodiacal jokes whereby they don't always let on but which keep their hearts in a constant state of jollity apart from the punishments their father metes out in time to prove that life is not all jokes all the way through. Tears or laughter, what does it matter after all! It's life that's the main thing. Yes. I suppose so but it's the cushion round the edge I want to put back, I the good for nothing (for everything). No more shall you attend my new universities to learn how to ridicule the weak and swindle them every which way and send them to their death and grab all their property which they've scraped together through sexual love or all kinds of decent work. Daddy allowed you some leeway for his leaven that is some soft purgatives to get rid of the toxic worms; but you revel in shit so much you want to hand it back to the others and get work as a joker that you've got used to purging the good and the bad alike be it with steel or poison. I'm not talking about your spiritualist intonations which draw gold spilling to your feet like the virgins you violate. You bring down accidents and fires through your power over all the acts of men and specially of women. What a shoddy mess it all is and yet somehow you're revered, petted, celebrated to the peak of human conceptions by its vital organization into associations which you disturb, manipulate, divide and divide afresh just to consolidate your absolute power which you want to live on for yourself, your disciples and your progeny, which equally asks only for that atmosphere that orgy of pleasure with not a single thought in mind for anything that doesn't contribute to fetching this overwhelming pleasure to its ultimate paroxysm. Mercilessly uncovered without the love of the next man and without the admittance to the faith of our spiritual advisor you'd be hung and quartered once they heard of your little ways. It's the man of feeling talking to you; one of those who's suffered more than enough in life without realizing at the time that it was you who were stealing all the elements of his happiness he was courageously seeking to establish. Even now you've still got him in your iron grip. You try to dope him with your worms and their nourishing stink, but you'll never get through to the soul: it'll always be stronger than anything you can muster. Take your hat off; and if in your heart you're not worthy to wear the scientist's hat at least have the guts to pick up a shovel, that'll teach you that as it gets used up, blood turns into sweat, but also that it's shit which as it's evacuated encourages the regeneration of the bodies which allow themselves to be fattened up like pigs that might as well stumble into the trough. Peck sailor you'll get the orange.

S. Lecocq

---

23.9.49. Rosalita. Rosalyta will tell you anything you want to know. But eye shitton yew toodle doo tweety mooch ooh lala. Tivvy tavvy tuv. Eyed door you the lady replied but furst eye knee two rhea shore mice selph bee 4 eye embraize your flame and test your fiddle itty. And don Joohoon so doted on his beauty with her bigbig eyes in a single burning kiss he made this sweet prom ice. Oh my Span nish bride eye sware it, this day you army eye doll and shall all ways bee so; for me in this life there can be nother hap piness and Donn Jooan my dar ling will key pew innis hart. If yury turn will you dare ask my par don and tell me why you winter way. I know 2 well that tall suffering is point less, I know what yule saigh if yury turn. Christ was nail down to his cross of infermee and from his ravv aged limbs the bludd pore fourth in streams, the tearz coarsing down his livid face his voice still sweet spoke to his tortu rers I scat turd seeds of love but half vested only hate, I pored fourth lighten two yore dark ness yet mercy lesley you low dead me down with heavy chains all though I brought you awly quality Hears dead dear god cried Marguerite thud ore is of eye ron it can nobby oh penned. Tizza terry bull dayfer the poor wee thing at this very mow meant she has her mother was dye ing. Once the forwards are in control the backs are there ready to back up any break throughs. They rein in swift and hard to keep up the advantage. They play off side for the over zealous and aim for touch when it's dicy. If they can't start anything they pass back to goal. The halves play in unison with their forwards and the backs like lightning resolute in dummies and feints which make sudden W's lightning waves short and long. The short extra is a swift pass by the forward line which is intent on scoring. Scoring a goal puts one over sheer muscle. The knew waves souldered for currants highly attractive it's an active resource hard to short-circuit. If it does the response should be the immediate joining of the two closest knots in front and the intermediary one. The whole secret of success lies in the strength the restraining force of the currant and its combined will power. For a currant to be highly productive it is ness ess erry for the acids to be adjusted to the accumes, so these last have no leaks, from normal sustained, usage and without any of that ox side which is a sure sign of age or faulty management.

comparison            S. Lecocq


Saint Jean de Dieu 12th August 1948.

Dear Doctor Bernard,

It's been almost seventeen months since I was confined to your esteemed doctoral intelligence. Having received from you in the way of treatment, in common with my fellow internees I may say, only the effluvia of your gaze eager to polish off the day's work in the same way you started it, I see no point in mincing words with an individual of your ilk. Just open up your memory or else my file and you will realize that Mr. Sylvain Lecocq is not the sort to attack anyone by stealth. You know full well the purpose which led me to Saint Jean de Dieu, which was to conduct a full-scale enquiry into what goes on in this place of caring rest and tranquillity, which has become the most odious establishment for incarceration in the entire world, under the guise of scientific bamboozlement, for eyes closed to knowledge, to education, and above all faith in God, the director of our souls which he guides at every moment, leaving it free too the individual to travel toward good or toward evil; even adding weight to the direction in which a being might incline. Your days as cynical manipulator of the weak are over. One of these last, whom like all the others you took to be a negligible lump good for nothing but providing a bit of spermi-cerebral nourishment for the delight of a few idle monarchs, has managed, over these past seventeen months of on the spot investigations, experienceing at first hand all the tribulations meted out by your diabolical powers, to lay bare all the barbaric medi evil practices which have been ceaselessly refined by hereditary exploiters, or else freshly promoted. Life in Saint Jean de Dieu is but an atom of what goes on amid the universal masses, it's only a question of weight by instinctual dissolution. My enquiries now having been completed my files comprising over a thousand pages handed over to those human elements which have retained their decency or are disgusted with the practices carried out in the name of a world wide progress which has long since been unmasked as the way to the pit, no organized force relying on mercenaries aware or unaware under the pressure of modern weapons whose value we know from A through Z by way of O, would be capable of suppressing that human energy hoodwinked for centuries and suffering today from famine from rumors of imminent massacre through preparations for war and from subverted faith. It is incumbent upon me to demonstrate to you my deductive powers so that you should be in a position to comprehend without being obliged to undergo an interrogation which might place too much strain on your poor brainbox. Let me say at once that we internees are all subject to hyperexcitation, being tended by people obsessed by love, perversity and sex. We are a special breed of farmyard animal and we've had our bellyful of being stuffed with promises, of being locked up, of being fed each day on contaminated human flesh, radio active food, meat from animals the abattoir turns away, along with all your hypnotic controls. To say nothing of the reserve stocks you've got stashed away in hiding places all of which I am perfectly capable of finding. So now you know exactly what to expect. The new institution which is already taking shape in the wings, and which will produce tangible results without spilling a single drop of blood, will not spare you the agony of being bound to the stake before a crowd which will surely rejoice to see devils burnt in accordance with God's decree. Doctor Bernard I inscribe here the fatal + which condemns you inexorably to the flames unless there be an immediate change of heart. This is your once and final warning. S.O.S. This letter as you will see has been signed by a number of entirely coherent internees who have penned their signatures after full and proper consideration.

Sylvain Lecocq

Maurice Delisle
Rambert Maurice
Léon Méru
Janssen Raymond
Ceroy G.
etc.

Did not sign: Chartrel, Desryel, Boucher, Hautecoeur, Duquesnoy, Blondel, Anne, Lemoine, Vandael.

Nine signatures out of 18 readers. That should be enough to demonstrate the mentality of certain humans who love things done to a nice turn thanks to their cowardly refusal of responsibility for their actions or their self-centeredness. This sort of cowardice exists in the selfsame proportions throughout the world.

TRANSLATED BY ROGER CARDINAL

SYLVAIN LECOCQ   Sylvain Lecocq was born of poor parents in Boulogne in 1900; he had little schooling but worked in commerce until, following an operation for a stomach ulcer in 1942 he could no longer work. He began to interpret his situation in a deranged manner and in 1947 was clinically certified. His file records an "active delerium with mystical themes." Interned at the Saint Jean de Dieu clinic, Lecocq made several escapes but was recaptured each time. In January 1950 Lecocq hanged himself from his bedstead with a length of bed-linen.

# BELGIUM

... they play with calm-natured people by making them rebel for nothing for silly things and if they make him rebel for ice cream for washing et caetera one must do this one must do that it's rebellion a little it's fine to see rebellion et caetera it happens all the time in the hospital et caetera he says they do that kind of thing almost eight years ago Monsieur Beril they do it together he says for eight years Monsieur Beril he persecutes me in my tastes because I have better taste than he which he always wants to intercept et caetera so that now all of a sudden I can't tell things the way they are that fifteen years with Monsieur Beril or fourteen years one can't remember this in an hour me I'm not Nostradamus he says but your tone goes to my heart because I'm like you I don't know how to answer you right away he said you speak softly now and you don't want to speak out loud kelanelsti-kikosti postirmaisi secret police of madmen secret police also to prove that the makalam of promakalam prokalastarrokalarems-brokelaisstrrmmakalaistostemarlokerster melaokester copy for me what you just said a national sick person Monsieur I would no longer know the spousk spousk spoukix of the marquise of Sevigne spousk why spousk spousix in the end he said that the brain registers just that and that good girls are good like you he said who have a normal character and heart who want to give you coffee when you ask for it but the rules don't allow it he said that yesterday we were really persecuted but here we're still at least among madmen who says Jacqueline why do you always speak of something else when I answer you well Monsieur this is why my question was the right one Cyrano de Bererac was it to pass the time because I can no longer de Bergerac Bergerac out loud siamur siamur siamur rassume before someone oarman reassume also small child who has never been to school who has not done this all that galumnied he says and why me I must speak like you he says since me I'm not like Marie du bas but then when you talk like that all alone you don't know how to say it you must scream through everything Monsieur it's so much war war is unjust he says because calm people they must ruin the nerves why he says because they are contrary natures they can do cruel things one sees them one always sees them rebel he says thas why thas why they possess the gift of language Monsieur in my brain it's pretty funny to say but you like very much to answer with your hands with your fingers that I recognize you well today and that if I don't love you I never loved you he says but I'm still charity in any case like you with the people that you like very much he says but me I don't love you I do my duty I was asked to do this or that and I can't say it that it's for your death he says that it's the truth he says that you well knew how to guess it but you now you can no longer look at anything what is it Jacqueline that has happened very well I think it's the blow I think it's the blow the woman downstairs gave me on the forehead I saw black for a third of a second it's not saw black but like a bar that possessed the gift of languages he said repeat after me again yes Monsieur without looking at me but of course Monsieur because me I look around like anybody else I don't look into eyes or into the face of someone I look at the whole when I speak to you but evidently with people one doesn't know very well when one is a little too close to explain oneself in that room nevertheless the house will be the same he says if I sit down like that and you a doctor but me I here's Monsieur I never liked doctors I don't like them because I've never been sick and I've never needed a doctor he says and that you don't know what a doctor is I don't like them Monsieur I hate them I find since what's been done to me I hate them and I hate the nurses too he says because you rebel and your salivary glands you should rebel to be fashionable he says and make other people laugh at you et caetera very well I'll make others laugh at you he

says I know very well how I should act you should be martyred
why because a saint is martyred too in his game he says they
have too good a figure for that I have too good a figure compared
to my sister he says but you nevertheless made the marquise of
Sevigne come down he said and people were not happy because
you acted like that but it was they themselves Monsieur in my
people phosphorescence on the youngish side like the school
teacher I do that to laugh with at my place little Henry come
here come here et caetera but never with a child and then I
never had children I don't like children I don't have the patience
no children who are not mine so little it's very normal he says
they have their mother me when little I have they took my
mother away I was eleven years old Monsieur and for eleven
years there that's the way it is and it's not otherwise that's the
way it is and then you'll have nothing and then that's the way it
is and then there and then there and then there and now forty-
nine years at last minus eleven years that that's the way it is I
know very well that you are normal he says and I like that too
but Monsieur me I adore my beauty shop equipment it's my
greatest love it's there that the worst crimes take place because I
had four little ones four or five it only cost three thousand francs
each it's only for the face for blackheads et caetera and then
when they rebelled with me they set off they saw flames et
caetera in the thing and I was very afraid eventually and I did it
for myself et caetera but that I nevertheless started again he says
that it can't badly it's done by specialists it can't badly electro-
cute I reassure the women who were afraid of electricity he says
but I know very well that it can't hurt anybody but they broke
and then I fixed a little and that now they promise to give the
things to Michele Beril from me and that she'll be more beautiful than I et caetera for eight years it's lasted Monsieur that this
that it's not the same kind that one doesn't reproach with
devaluration like that devaluration devaluration what is that

what is that I know very well what I'm saying but devaluration it's not the same value as you Jacqueline since there are twenty years difference but why choose that girl to give me shit that I never said that word either and for a year that I've been there then in rue Pommier not a year but still one can't calculate just like that on the spot it will be for her each time that I loved something it's for ah Odette the same size the same breadth each time I got dressed but I see here Monsieur my disposition made me fight those people and I hate those people I don't like them any more don't bring them near me any more I did nothing wrong to them and I wasn't made to take advantage of my youth it's Monsieur Beril who introduced me like that she is nice she likes to laugh or things like that this taste to have me accepted in my rue Vivegnis apartment and make me accept those people who must eat together all together and must be together and as soon as I was seated Monsieur to telephone mama telephone mama but I too Monsieur I suffered indirectly [from here on Jacqueline sobs until the end] oh mama said this and then me I am not obliged to listen to this I want to finish with him when he is always like that Monsieur. . . . I understand very well too because I am not stupid Monsieur that I understand it all that which they have it's to attack indirectly because they see that I don't know how to speak I don't know how to speak with people who don't interest me Monsieur and then I am not a great talker aside from my business it's the most beautiful day of my life that I lived with my Insititute of beauty Monsieur and then to dress myself it's the only thing that interests me but I am all alone Monsieur why I went thinking to give my things that I so loved and that I love still so much why I must give my things to others that I don't have because he will die and all that and always to die they will die and have their nerves shot those who are calm to hear the tables of voices et caetera the vocal chords of artists et caetera Marie from downstairs et caetera the others too he says but that's why when you make obligatory exchanges it rings a little like that Monsieur now my mouth dries out like the Jesus Christ of the church he's the greatest martyr in the world and there never was a good Lord Monsieur it's the others who are there superior forces that my sister asked me one day you know that something happened I no longer know what there are superior forces but one dosen't know what that is and I cried Monsieur are the assassins and he knew very well that it's true but that to bother me they rebelled so that I might have a softer tone or I don't I don't know what they said about vocal chords that evidently I know to say what even to Monsieur Beril even when I want to speak it doesn't interest him drink a whiskey with me it doesn't interest him with him he doesn't like whiskey he drank it in the past he was happy he was unhappy he wasn't happy I ask him what he wants nothing comes out of his mouth Monsieur me I prefer someone frank it hurts perhaps but it's said it's said if he had said now Jacqueline I can't keep you here any longer et caetera and who would have told you listen since me my greatest happiness I have judged now that he would have explained well I would have left but with my equipment Monsieur with my instruments too fifteen years ago it comes back perhaps thirty thousand francs et caetera he says.

TRANSLATED BY SOPHIE HAWKES

JACQUELINE   Born in Belgium in 1918, she eventually settled in Brussels where she opened a beauty parlor. She remained unmarried, but at the age of 38 she moved in with a Mr. Beril, who was divorced, and with his two children. She fought frequently with Mr. Beril, whom she blamed for the failure of her business. The text presented here is the result of a recording made by a doctor of statements made in

December of 1967 at the Brugmann hospital in Brussels, where she was interned at the time. She is now "cured."

## MARMOR

### 1 - 8 - 51—THE 55TH DAY OF
### MY SOLITARY CONFINEMENT

Memory of my stay in a so-called Rest home designated formerly as the ex-camp of Luzerne, one from Luzerne, renamed since 1852 "Fool's Paradise," happy and mulnerable are the real disciples there or direct descendant of the Crupper of Aliboron the Wise; Loony candidate if they are merely men in good health, but "uninquirily" sick unaware of themselves like Everybodyelse.—It's not I who say this it but an operetta Doctor, "Doctor Knock" . . . the Queen muse must have touched the author with her royally-sincerely and justly inspiring wing:

A few rhymes well rhymed written without the foot cult 1300 years ago says Dr. Ley, a humorist by fancy are equally like me at Mr Delporte's place, lucubrist inconstall and imbalanced balancing act install like me (Know) by definition meaningless to the Delporte man.

Laurent Pichat turning
Big blow
Strikes Empis
next, Empi—staggering
Coward says
Bah! too bad!
lucubrations like those of an
excellent psychiatrist

only one worthy of the name
a fool for whom "Nyet" is from
an unknown and viperous language.

---

1st Marmoric lucubration
according to unknown author, retained and transcribed for pos-
terity by Undersigned (Dr Ley) intended for the survivor Marmor takes the liberty of continuing in his opinion the thought of
this petrified author, carbon should probably already do it.

Continued by the patient already
so happy!!! to see grandma
with whom ardent ex-sunset
in time, alas! and becoming
however in thinking about the grandmother:
I am an ex- young guy and ardent grandfather
However, grand fa-first class already?
But let's pigprickish it well "that way
it about-ships by itself and more but I'm afraid
And it would truly be a shame, more than anything
to be the cuntcubine, of a grandmother
intoxicating-ly no it would be too bitter.
And I prefer even to this next humiliation
To write the life story of a certain wordly Doctor Sow
Singlehandedly giving birth to fourteen little Demans.

Next scene in the oyster* room, if the thinble Good order chief-
buttock less sly less re-versatile, moore dick-tation à la neder
throws at the bottom of Do—polopiqued at all hours of the day
in the perojactive sense, very very softly to cuntserve my dick-
tation in the Gorrect sense and well washed night until the (rear)
end of the day—you have time to rest with my sick people

sixteen and six younger sons of their fathers who were not nightwatchmen either! sus ka!

> Silence, Misstterr Marrshalll, we're ffffilming
> Muzhik Maestro quett. vous piss? (Already?)

The national spaaker enters entranced upon the obscene scene obsequating toward a micron broad as these two show-elders so far ap art, tonitruanting already in a vicarial voyse, parodying p . . . light in his 45 × 80 ten in size, the schoolboy voice reciting his last prayer before the strike of S.M. Leroy only prolix with the packer-lady with the pachyderm rebounded and with a pearly belly with an elastic strategy; veritable mother for her beloved younger son, handsome fello who says, to his arms, leaning towards her purple and cunning lips, "Mama I adore you! But me Toot great herring Booby—I will undo you no later than tonight while Papa reads the little evening advertisements for an uncertain tomorrow, looking for work that is "e - z - to - wax"—I love you Oh oh me my fat future crowned pig, from which I'll have a son! It's your mamama who's telling you this already . . . How Cuntfessed mamorous Mama . . . I'll teach you on first loins' thrust my dear little mork! Careful! papa pricks his eyes! let me go I'm suffocating already just thinking of the skinscape of this sleepless night—Must I really? But of course! big morceau: my first fall I shall always come down in the arms of the family Then all's well.

---

2nd lucubration
Swan and (Ley) on plan six
rat-skinning, harsh it's 13
without years in forgetting
What Memoring! pissy cast-rating

spreeing-yews, tiresome
depends not counting slakement
lies with lyes, marqueening
to all comers, bleating stupidly;
Hard-ly, its Rossellant and Pascally devout
But in re-nun-ciation of this seer
Nigra gent'lemen-lover soule an-sir-ring
After the bury-all of his 50%
This miri-agent not litering
tiring this second lout
lover discovering, not furrowing,
believing in his hilarant, charming
God—Truly do you know Lout?
who cherishing child stupidly weeping;
very clairvoyant a bout peep all rite now in the fur row
marrying his 10 or 8 years priesting meting a prince charming
who was but a guttersnipe lowlife
niting all the time but not for long and seldom talking!

Pst! Miss! don't count
the feet! one could be
missing and you wouldn't be able
to stand up the last
[illegible]
of the too tight spring.
again of a sudden
after discharging
so tiring.

3rd lucubration**
Childbirth Without Mid-wife-fermentaling neither quickly

and rhinairy glauticous influsion in the stables without rhining
namhing the swelling feet coming all
(And neither tell anyone if you please or R.I.2 threatening)
Now then! Once upon a time not long age:
Doctor Laie thinking of the disgusting "worming" that made
him suffer so atrociously, in this moment of laboring agushment,
copiously, male reckoning just many female animals and maling
not a single one! it's enraging! but he went about it so awkwardly
this long filthying, gasping his male cuntentment in trances of
piggishness! Next in one or two years, the cuckolding, freely, I'll
laugh a long time! new beau thinking kindly of my contentment
so ante that he thinking however! Then continuing, hatching
tirelessly, enumerating with difficulty these remains, meanwhile,
a suckler already, greedily, but still awkwardly, their Mama,
bitterly farrowing; nevertheless the hanging bellying; Deflating
however, but not enough for contentment. Continuing courageously in rocking the suckler; thinking left-handing right, thinking left, so scratching the grung bling much material meninging
reflection. Philosophically Scarifying, story-smiling without
however hearing. Without Cunt viction here-ply there is say! 14
ruminating quadraplants under there there inside.—86 bones of
smoking hams greasily drying, but stinkhing right now one
couldn't more disagreably the apartment, Mama's moving out.

---

. . . eleven shush or cunt-speak (So! I was saying . . . but what was
I saying in moving out on the subject of this pontificating,
terrifying Papa?—
   Oh, Voché: this third-echo with the crushed rescue-dog's
rubric; this mata-sudden and prompt death at the re-tort fat and
low who can't close the debit of his scalding hot water faucet and
its sluice principally in the rear of the tran onthefloor below toss

tender age when his wicked ventripolent debiting alarming
groans going outside the remains of his clothing amply, nar-
rowly, measuring the pedant; splitting his own sides in the x'ces
wind vans ran-tan-plan, with sitting ducking steps slowing
perusing strong smelling nosymanaging cunt-currents, fleeing
the wind nose-forward, forward march! forward march. Ran . . .
tan . . . plan. plan plan . . . Psoftly psalmodizing the bury-all
now's the time, hens-fourth, next, the last plan slanting the bad
man towards the fields where everyone in scramming will spill a
touching, tear-jerking, clairvoyant Go in Praise while signing a
blest +! so soothing it will chase and purr-sue the last follower
the diligent ditchdigging hurried rapscallion finishing the burial
by tossing the necessitating earthing Elisawise defi-native-ly.
Amen.

But why! Damn, have I caused the (too) err-ly death of that
commissioner so goodly a lady with others' children and no
sources of water of non-trouts seedated and yet so prettily
adorned.

And thus the resus-citation for a half-time (mi.temps). Thus
the stomach split-sleeping in the Wind that worries it, chasing
and pursuing ex-crements creamy and pointed, creamature and
creamating. Or-dorizing the bed's sheeters in the middle of
Halve-time.—

Getting up, rushing, blessing, cursing, hastily, feverishly ad-
justing the indecent, smelly pendants; not managing it except by
putting a dressing-screen in front; sealing up an independent
countersession regrettably less shocking now; brandishing in
time, many long years ago, more than fifty and some half-years;
currently lowering the lamen-table-lee; dripping and marking
time, lightly marching, skipping about almost better than a
"climber," not flying but "sailsetting" as in the Goodoldays,
almost now, pleasantly remembering that good time, ridiculing
those following because being young (year) not knowing the

"meanwhile" to his detriment, because he was 20 or 30 years old!! ; Often tottering arriving blowing, suffering before the apartment's plan reading, deciphering with difficulty because of his age and hee-haw forcing his limping advance, the placement of this closed clan seen sitting on its seat, aiming poorly in the remainder of its smelly deliquescent nourishments heavily on the side-ways nose; Ending his hencefortifying outpourings, getting up less painfully, getting dressed again less painfully, young outside this time with dignity, resuming his advance, his plans, directing himself more cheerfully, more lively than before, before the ad-dressing screen; Storming, smiling as before of course, still tracing while skipping less surely, following his prudent references but still just as disgusting.—Reaching his destination, leering at the halve-time middle of his hole made by his unseemly seeming, impressing his spanking giants; creating a draft of stale but agitated air itself agitating, dessicating, abridging that humidifying rheumatizing naughty man in the extreme for the imprudent ones, the patients lying in this naughty rigid folder.

Calling desperately, going back to bed immediately; abusing the absent orderly, ordering or confirming thus the rule of internal order; who, having finally come, cursing ripping patient, undressing unfolding oozing still more, like the delinquent's seemliness; wiping here, lashing there, shaking the fracas of sheetholders like the unhappy patient; hiccuping at the heavy bottom of a very recent penetrating rest, angering all the way inside me with "dessicating radiant, decolorizing, vaporizing, dessicating all that was there inside.

Coming back from the bathroom white as though coming back from the other world, coming and vomiting on the sheet-ends, at that instant, of the still deliquescing but repentant deliquent; uselessly repeating to so many louts comprising the lunatics' room, bedwetting sheetshitting voluntary hibernators necessarily sanely referred as healthy but possessing money, Kings of the injected, emperor of ex-madmen, Knight of the feather in the Winds of cold nights, threatening yet coming home, from the phenomenant MARMORANT sorcerer's apprentice, bewitching all the personnel who know the Marshall plan and his homonymy curiously attracting dominating all the uprights to gloomy room 8, pseudonimating under the chestnutty MARMOR IN a box jailing even that rapscallion, his male and female overseers, striking dead even Frida chief worse-nurse all this saying that damned Marshall shoesmith, wishing him damned and for a long time! I hope.—

All these people stuffing their no-says-in-the-err, eating discreetly according to this fulminating constant derangement, the condiments, before the accident hanging from the nose of every old and newcomer, even recalcitrant, mocking ones, momentarily but for a long time. The incident now quieting, the cuntpanions withdrawing to their half-restful folders; digesting while thinking that the food, however nourishing, is often discunt-serting for the non-ruminating bi-pedant, farting while waiting; sleeping, daydreaming, crying fearfully but cheerfully for nothing, thinking of the poor fool of the accident; at the bed's turnabout no ting complaining still timidly softly, lightly but only snorings now, breathing while whimpering very softly; finally escaping, they think, the punishments of the ghosts returning from the closed bathroom clan mocking the building of xcessive madmen, miscreants and other debonair bad men justifying his missing money but only in his bank account, and awaiting the ressurection so the repentants giving back the treasure of the depositor involuntarily, by wicked procedure having been applied with little decency however:

Let us await the punishment of the returning ghosts bleating their inconveniently; passing ahead of the follower, wrangling the belly-floppers coming home subsequently in order to be before the supreme judging though arbitrarily though happening the male unseemly crunchers wallowing while beseeching that they didn't want to be before, they themselves judging unseemly while crunching and eating Satan's coins before they gave them horns themselves.

Amen! Year 1000 nine hundred and fifty and one year, the 13th of the month bloing Janu-airy in the erra of Jesus Christtan.

Sign MARMOR STILL living and bellyaching voluntarily.

TRANSLATED BY SOPHIE HAWKES

NOTES:

* Above this line on the top of the page Marmor drew a sow on a bed, suckling a pig, looking right towards a nurse lying down exposing her breasts and her genitals. The scene is captioned, "Oyster room—pissers' corner, metallic mattress filtering always dry, never washed, always Glean." The sow says in a bubble, "LEAVE ME I'LL GET OUT OF IT ALONE, vack to your OQP in bitt alleys mauling while waiting for you dear FRIGID FRIDA." The nurse responds, "HELP! SEND ME THE PRICK MEN! OH! DON'T PASHA! I PREFER PIG MEN I SAY TO YOU ALWAYS AND TOTALLY HARMED."

** This piece is again illustrated by a sow giving suck to a young pig, and it has the partially unreadable words, "Pile of great deeds nothing ork. Especially leave nothing while leaving no rabbids and frogs borne in corners on the ceiling like Dupont. Get the hell out of here therefore in too good health in this [illegible] dwelling. What a chicken I am!! One, two . . . thirteen said the Veterruinarian lepolling and suling on his pawings. Come then and hang on black worse too swelling it's heavy such weight disappearing from my paralyzed swelling which reading already for such a long time."

MARMOR    Nothing is known for certain about this author (who gave himself the pseudonym of "Marmor") except that he was interned in a Belgian psychiatric hospital, where he composed his three "lucubrations" in January of 1951.

# AUSTRIA

## HOPE

The grace of a woman.
The will for beauty
Cleverness, Hope.
Hope, Luck.
My shoe pinches a lot.
Hope squeezes the heart.
The heart hurts.
It is always Death.
The beauty to Hope.

## THE FACE

The face is sometimes round
and sometimes longish.-
Loyalty is in the eyes.
the nose is in the middle.
the mouth. The face.
people and everyone has
        a face.
The face is the first thing
    that catches man's eye.

## THE SKY

The sky is blue.
The stars are gold.
The clouds are white.
It has always been that way.

The sky is over the clouds.
The sky is beautiful.
The sky is high.
and I wouldn't stay in the sky.
The sky is here.


## THE PSYCHIATRIST

The psychiatrist takes care of
                the patient.
The psychiatrist thanks and thinks
                about the patient.
The psychiatrist thinks and protects
                the words of the patient.


## POETS

The greater the suffering
The greater the poet
The harder the work
The deeper the meaning


## JOY AND SUFFERING
(based on Goethe)

It is really difficult to live. Pain.
Pain, pain! It grieves one to death.
Is that love ! ?
Life.—

## THE DREAM

The dream is a playful game
of the night - a sleep. For one
Person.- It is actually a present
from another person. At night! ——


## JOY

Joy and anticipation
Joy comes from the heart.
Anticipation is an idea -
A coming together - mind and eye.

TRANSLATED BY CLAUDIA STOEFFLER


ERNST HERBECK (pseudonym "Alexander") was born in 1920 in Stockerau, Austria. Since 1946, he has lived at the Gugging Institute. He has had several works published, including a book, *Alexander: Selected Writings 1961-1981* (in German). His poem "The Sword" was published in 1989 in the Partisan Review. (Courtesy Dr. Leo Navratil)

# GERMANY

EDITOR'S NOTE:  The final selections are taken from an anthology of written works in the Prinzhorn Collection (*Leb wohl sagt mein Genie: Ordugele muss sein,* 1985, edited by Inge Jádi) and translated by Peter and Sarah B. Hoffmann with the kind permission of Verlag das Wunderhorn, Heidelberg, Germany. The "biographies" following the writers' work are those provided by the Prinzhorn Collection. With their flat labels of "schizophrenic" and "dementia praecox" and the like they suggest some of the limitations of traditional assessment of the "insane" and their creative work.

## INTRODUCTORY ESSAY
## BY FERENC JÁDI

THE PRINZHORN Collection is an internationally renowned documentation of creative works of the mentally ill at the University of Heidelberg's Psychiatric Clinic. The collection consists of some 6,000 objects: drawings, pictures, collages, textiles, sculptures, books and notebooks as well as hand-written texts, produced between 1880 and 1933 mainly by hospitalized schizophrenic patients in various institutions.

According to editor Inge Jádi, only a small fraction of this material has been made public, mostly in the volume that is widely regarded as a standard work on the subject, *Bildnerei der Geisteskranken, (Imagery of the Mentally Ill,* Springer Verlag, 1922).

The collection had its beginnings in plans for a psychopathological museum intended as a research facility, with the interest centered on the visual works of expressions by the mentally ill. It had started with a questionnaire mailed out in 1919 by Hans Prinzhorn, an art historian, psychologist and medical doctor, who wrote to major institutions mostly in the German-speaking parts of Europe describing the project and asking for appropriate contributions.

Prinzhorn's appeal met with a great deal of success. Together with the visual art material, a great number of handwritten documents were received which were included more or less accidentally as additional documentation and which Prinzhorn regarded as such.

Prinzhorn made reference to only a few of these texts in certain contexts. It is not surprising that the existence of these texts, which make up an important part of the collection, was practically unknown until quite recently.

The criteria guiding the selection of the texts included, first, their breadth and variety which were intended to provide a notion of the patients' real situation inside the institution; second, identity of language and person, i.e. an indication of how languages leave the human being; and third, the unity of the written image and its expression.

TRANSLATED BY PETER AND SARAH B. HOFFMANN

INGE JÁDI worked as a physician at Heidelberg University's Psychiatric Clinic from 1972 to 1975. Since 1975 she has been custodian of the Prinzhorn Collection there. She has written in specialized journals and in catalogues about the collection.

FERENC JÁDI has worked as psychiatrist and as poet in Hungary. He has written many publications in the area of psychiatry and art. Since April 1985 he has been assistant at Heidelberg University's psychiatric clinic. Presently, they live in Berlin.

# ERNST BERNHARDT

My Dears!

Acute agitations alternate with halusions.* - Every moment an excitation of the senses, a vision of the senses. - Like the last ones. I am my own psychiatrist. You don't have to give in to any fears, that I am here is my own will, as everything else bends to my will. It's all an exercise. More tomorrow. I am already very tired now, and I would have to force myself if I wanted to keep on writing as above, because I don't have the strength to be active in one direction, additionally the fountain pen costs more than 3 [. . .] and the nib is no Roesles nib.** Thus, one rushes too much what one can't force. I am my own king, and subject only to the German emperor. Farewell, I am healthily says my geniusily. I haven't sentily the latest poem as yet. Wallily has it and wants to keep it but I can't marry her because she is stupid as the night. Please to take me to another cow-shed the next time. I am not going to let me and my kind get stuck with such a pack rat; that's the last time I'm going to tell you that. When you visit me, then you will come to me and me alone. I am no little jerk but a strictly knowledge-thought-through head who kindly refuses any annexation and who asks you to come to me alone each time and no bats cryingeling to me. You know exactly what I want to say. But I have you, forgive me. Thou wert to . . .*** and in reverse principle farewell says my genius orderly must be. You recognize from my way of writing that I am neither ill, nor healthy but just am & I write only with Roesles nib 3 [. . .] fountain pen. After all we want to stay good friends. I can't reproach myself or anyone else, I know now that Zichler is a stupid gent and if he thinks it takes a million to quit the state church then he is an ass the likes of which the world, as long as it exists, hasn't seen. Now and then I have to go really fast and then

**191**

go slowly again right away. [. . .] In spirit farewell don't show the letter to anybody my genius doesn't want it, you see that I am sick, otherwise I wouldn't have [. . .] and very left in and out, but would have written regularly. For a good farewell, a genius doesn't have to be a school master. I'm Dr. Ironbeard,**** I say, and cure people in my own way***** me

Ernst

TRANSLATOR'S NOTE:
* Apparently a contraction of "hallucinations" and "illusions."
**A brand name presumably.
***Unclear abbreviation.
****German: Dr. Eisenbart.
*****This is the beginning of a German folk rhyme: *Ich bin der Dr. Eisenbart, und kurier' die Leut nach meiner Art.*

ERNST BERNHARDT   Dementia praecox; copy of a handwritten transcript of a letter, 1908.

## ELSE BLANKENHORN

IN THE FOX-DEN
A SPIRIT FLOWS
BUBBLING
ON SUNNY
HEATH UNDER
THE SELF A
SMALL CHILD LIES
SAD IN
BLACK
DRESS

LITTLE WILM
I ~~DIDN'T~~
~~LIKE~~ YOU
R FATHER
BECAUSE HIS
SOUL WAS NOT
WITH LITTLE
~~EDITH~~ BUT RATH
R IN THE
GOLDEN
LAND OF
LOVE -


THE KISS

The attraction of a person foranother
is radiance of love. Toanother

Jesu says, the kiss is the seal
of man in plight.

ELSE BLANKENHORN   Schizophrenic; from a book with drawings and text, undated.


# WILHELM MUELLER

DEATH

Hermit alone unassum
ing
        Phil. o. Schol.

Saint in life
        e.g.
        Practical
        1. music
  Art    2. painting
        3. poetry
Philosophy  1. Philosophy a. cultural ideas
             b. metaphysics and natural
                philosophy and religions
        2. Holiness      mythical
          noble, serious, decent, peaceful,
          friendly, well-meaning, among people
        No vanity, sensuality! Starving.

Means for that: Mentally: Character, brains, spirit, religion; freedom. Perfection, truth.

I do not want to run away! because I can demand, as educated and learned man, that I be released. I want to wait for that. Until then, paint an oil painting; then lie quietly in bed and wait, to gather new thoughts and expect a cure.

Yes, it is good, if

Participants! All
        of them
        Count Leopold v. Kalkreuth, painter; poetry
        B. Military man

A Genius is he who lives for the best of his own self and of mankind, to fulfill the custom, to replace, with God's help, one idea with another and that is a struggle!

II.
Now I see with sorrow, way in back

the forest rustles and the waves
of the lake move in the reeds.

WILHELM MUELLER    Schizophrenic; excerpt, undated.


# MAX ZIERL

## THEATER

(What is otherwise the job of the director: the facilitation of the
dialogue among the relevant persons, that everybody can relate
to himself the words heard by him, is achieved here by the
indirect language and language of the emotions:)


OUTSIDE:

The Outcast: "Salvation is via. . . !"

The Poet: (as he moves closer from the distance:) "The out-
cry. . . !" - "a modern one!" "A cry for help!" "in a military sense
simple and understandable; because there are such trains in
time of war; railroad trains: "Friends! Here! Help!"

The Outcast: "In the end there is. . . !"

The Poet: "My poetry!" (He has seen the outcast)

The Telephone, Gliding Past: "That's the way it is!"

The Outcast: "Show yourself! It pleases fate, to put in a word.
The judge is nearby; because my spirit's friend
recognizes the twin of his nature." (spirit = twin:

the indirect language.) "The novelty of being keeps
the demon away from the threshold of our Eden, and
gladly appears as spirit-twin, which was lamented
wholeheartedly. Nowhere is there absolute life, and
its holiness gives me strength, for the dignity of action.
A spirit comes over me, that sunny fare: the
sensual desire of male wishes. Religion's guest
listening to poems whisper, finds the humanity's
friend in the circle of the living, conveying the
intimacy of the subconscious in order to befriend
the questioning notion."

The Telephone: "The great spirits are born, hour by hour."

The Outcast: "The Whole consists of today and tomorrow. The
future is the leader of pride, which loves the
human being as a justification, and that provides
to each his own. Because that which is near only
grants a delay of the shadow of fate, because the
uncertain does not fit into everything. The
language of the Indirect gathers moments of the
Self instead of the Direct. On the whole, a man;
the gathering hour is: "to the day, today!"

The Telephone: "Leadership = Poetry!"

The Poet: "The creative sensitivity takes the telephone,
and the "master" is the new old man of the poet.
If the showing is the world for us, life whispers
language to the senses. If you are you for yourself, listen to the elf at the beginning. If the
Nearby is the world, the poet disappears, comet-
like, in the clouds of others whose souls take off
the mask of the inconsequential during the dance of
the spirit. The Unknown appeals to him. Friends =

spirits bring into the triumph of position love of
affairs. The thinking Other is based in the circle
of the change of persons, male glory displays the
web of friendship as salutes to the arrivals. The
relationship catches the man in order to poison the
experienced ladies for the children of paradise.
Circumspection lends reality to the service,
and on it relies the poetry of the welcoming
world, disclosing itself in beautification."

The Outcast: "An increase in the feelings of tension in the
enemy . . . ?" "Performance = preparation . . . ?"
"Action is the necessity of the Clear, and I grant
the Telephone the fact, which guides the feeling
of comprehension of these relationships. Here,
the Telephone aligns with . . ."

The Poet: "The Fact counts on the Doing" "Shape of things,
follow me!"

Junior Officer: "We count on ourselves, because the justification
for this is our attitude."

The Outcast: "We like ourselves in our security, and nevertheless, pressures ripen me in wide requirements. . . ."

Junior Officer: "with a program of the state church. The lot of
the beautiful is a territorial law. I promise myself the point of view of overcoming by the truth
of action. The mixture of happiness colors the lot
of coming generations. Telegramm: "Notifications"-
"We"-"For man man"-that then is the slogan of
choice: Before going, the generalities." "The
abbreviating terseness is self-access!"

Lord of the Cloister: "Humanity sends greetings to mankind by
the prevention of an illness. The group = spirits send
greeting to man by the creation of gold. Group =
artists, the church, sends man greetings through
the church. The elf of the awakening of a friend
declares the truth for me. The Judgment of Mildness
in this is the church. For man: greetings through
the institutions, and heaven strengthens the mild
loan!"

Junior Officer: "The conspirit, the comet comes with the prayer;
disappears with it, takes the measure closer to
Greatness." -Telegram: "the coming was like this"-
"yesyes, the thing itself - the things are often
the no!" - "Are: order we:"

Senior Officer: "are reports here." "The good thoughts are
standing by; we think them around the forehead.
The telephone puts the words in. The fact in-
cludes the doing. Fantasy is the most silent of
reality. The judgment: in the excellence of the
individual - and we are careful. The ladies are
entering . . ."

Local Ladies: "In investigating the history of suffering of the
interests, the ideal of the beauty of fate emerges.
Shadow feelings envelop the errors of the impression = barbarian, who colors the joys of life."

4 Ladies: Lady in Blue: "The woman patriot serves everyone
personally."
Lady in Red: "Everybody serves the lady member of an order."
(Lady member of an order)
Lady in Green: "Everybody serves even the proven lady."
(Proven Lady)

Lady in Violet: "He serves everybody."
(Everywhere)

Local Lady: "Said lady is privy to the life dreams of world reason."

Lady in Blue: "Happiness comes only rarely," is a merchant's sentence. "We greet millions in love."

Lady in Red: "Those farthest away from home draw nearer to each other under one color. This, generally, is red."

Lady in Green: "The women don't go into details. They articulate in general sentences. The green presides in the color play of flowers as examining world."

Lady in Violet: "The sun gives the dewey gloss to sadness. It becomes a sun-rainbow. This Everywhere gives the reconciled, generally; because the deprivations are admired only by the church."

The Outcast: "Confidence gives itself to the people again in form of the new. The circle of ladies interested in life is ours, and they command with the opinion of the good."

Senior Offlcer: "You name for us the personality. . . ."

Local Lady: "The strangeness from the men's world indicates the non-virtue of overrating. Woman's memory leads the way like an elm to summon up the service = messengers for the elven = dance of the culture = beings, which deserve the old opinion."

First Lady: "Give some hints to the tender. Reason does not detract from woman; because the beautiful is hers, and in the existing she honors the search."

Second Lady: "We will come in good time. This for once - and we consider ourselves as needed."

Third Lady: "Here the precondition was valid in its entirety of the own for the prescience."

Fourth Lady: "To you". . . .

The Outcast: "For the workers, this word is a judge. The command is the instruction for the others."

Worker: "Becoming the master will come to us. Many things are accomplished by honor. The King is the firm = hand. We think of it as the forehand. The rebellion in law is an objection to the order. The conditions of suppression represent the angle, until we shape it into a rectangle. Beautiful people - beautiful workers. The ladies' world has been able to cope with them. The nourishment is peace. The know-how on top, and we strengthen the stronghold of labor."

Police Agent: "Here, service plays a role, and the Furthermore justifies what's mine" - was the slogan for the day. The "Stillfort" is, like the night rain on the site of the apparition = electricity, which here leads to beauty."

MUNICH, NOVEMBER 1894

INSTRUCTIONS.

Based on these instructions, some of the strangest manifestations of modern society are passing by here in rhetorical form. The strangest of these manifestations: the outcast - somebody resurrected by heavenly grace concentrates in himself the transitions of the language of passion, and this until they tum to the new ladies' point of view. This ladies' world itself, as well as the other phenomena demonstrated here, move outside the sequence of phenomena if the rectangular point of view = and manner of speaking impart such a certain significance in themselves that they must necessarily rearrange themselves for reality in some sort of larger societal form: thus, the theater is over for those depicted here in this treatise; those society types expounded here now step in the realm of heaven or earth, in other words: into the church or the state. The ambiguity of the language of passion, confirmed and emphasized now by the telephone is for theater speech that what used to be called: the humor of the theater; now one calls this the telephone service; thus, for example, the first sentence: "Salvation is via. . . ! - is for the outcast a question of time - for the poet, representing the public at this moment, it can be this sentence: it can be an indication, that a military train actually went by, as such trains can have such a character, and as the poet who appears here, actually interprets it that way until he spots the outcast, seeing in him the final representation of his poetry, which now stirs up sympathy for a time, like any poetry, telephone and passion impulses in their new formulation. And it is similar with the other sentence formations and sentence expressions.

MAX ZIERL    Schizophrenic; from 'bundle' with texts and drawings, 1894.

## HELENA PHILOMENA KLARA
## KATINKA MAISCH

Satellite and Comet had a dispute about the illuminating power of the sun's rays. Two snakes which contain the waves of the ocean in order to prevent the flooding of the land, hear about this dispute. They circle the earth, deprive her of the poison. The earth loses her gravity. Land and people are drawn out of the world's orbits. Because of this a noise arises on the earth, giving Poliphemus the sense of hearing. Poliphemus wants to collect these tones, and Euphrosyne, who examines the earth with a sounding lead, comes for that reason. They decide to build a marble city. Its inhabitants, fed at a single table on whose marble surface a dove appears every year which follows the call of the pelican. The color image is assembled by 12 council members. Poliphemus who knew the light long before the sense of hearing, adjusts the sun's spectrum. With this knowledge, a journey into the sea is decided on. The new world is to gaze at the heavens in lighter colors.

Helena Maisch<br>F.U. 1

Sanatorium near Konstanz, February 1920.

HELENA PHILOMENA KLARA KATINKA MAISCH   Schizophrenic; text with drawn elements on the back page of a drawing, 1920.

## OSKAR HERZBERG

Three fishermen:   (trio!)   the dragon is coming!
Head fisherman:   Siegfried is coming!   (tenor!)
three fishermen:   (trio!)   the dragon is coming!
Head fisherman:   Siegfried is coming!   (tenor!)
three fishermen:   (trio!)   the dragon is coming!
Head fisherman:   Who says it then?   (tenor!)
three fishermen:   (trio!)   he's already here!
Head fisherman:   Who says it then?   (tenor!)
three fishermen:   (trio!)   he's already here!

Head fisherman:   Who says it then?   (tenor)
three fishermen:   (trio!)   he'll devour us, yeah
Head fisherman:   Siegfried is coming!   (tenor)
three fishermen:   (trio!)   he'll devour us, yeah
Head fisherman:   Siegfried is coming!   (tenor)
three fishermen:   (trio!)   his native land is Asia!
Head fisherman:   Siegfried is coming!   (tenor)
three fishermen:   (trio!)   Victoria!
Head fisherman:   Siegfried is coming!   (tenor)
three fishermen:   (trio!)   Victoria!
Head fisherman:   back into the woods!   (tenor)


EXPLANATION OF THE END OF THE WORLD

On April 3, 2053 due to the collision of the ice comet with the comet Bila; main comet in uncalculable distance on the western horizon; sun, moon, stars pale; fall vertically into endless night.

Oskar Herzberg
Director General at the Royal Nerve Clinic in Leipzig

2-16-1914

---

Dissertation about night flight out of Aetna happens once annually only the night 3-11; led by Lucifer; everyone without distinction received no shirt; allowed to take along one child; enveloped in smoke and fog cloud; circle parts of the earth; the train to work disappears into Aetna; painter (is) eye witness; hypnosis convinces; riding along permitted

Sincerely Oskar Herzberg

1-6-1914

## DESCRIPTION OF A BEAR ATTACK

On old country road from Regensburg to Munich two men are striding; to shorten the way cut through the forest; barely left the road, both see right under an oak a runaway large fullgrown black bear resting on moss; they think he has died, walk right up to him; the hungry monster immediately gets up, growls with stretched neck at two frightened men; in fear both climb up nearby tree; beneath claws right paw, pulls the man down by his boot; mangles and bites into right arm, chews full hour on his feed, until only bloody bones remain of unlucky victim.

Oskar Herzberg

---

Describe an equestrienne whom see 1865 in Berlin Tiergarten dash back and forth, lady dismounts at Brandenburg Gate, steps up, gaze at full-bodied dapple-grey horse, in passing dubious equestrienne pronounced energy, which causes me to ask short question, her name Emy Dalman, lives for the time being at Doenhof Square in same building where hear my star Pauline Lucca precious singing, unfortunately curtain, pulled shut by cord, destructively dashes my hopefulness.

Oskar Herzberg

---

"Explain wedlock; you should live in a small house; save in time so you have in need; buy lockable money-box; a modest firm deliver furniture; remove alcohol; be forgiving in argument and fight is better getting along than hitting; remove lecherous house friend; do not be jealous; splinters matrimony; if you do not marry a woman cook, buy cookbook; buy chips from a sawmill for winter; demand waste blocks at 1 mark per centner, burn only wood, take time for that; sell ashes; order 1 centner a week; not overheated; the fire starts up in 2 minutes; don't let it smolder; put matches high up; children often smoke the cane, I myself try cigar made by uncle Bauer by rolling it with fingernails, I got sick, throw up; tell in school, children tattle to teacher Doerfer; (with half-hard breadroll); receive 25 counts on behind from principal Ramshorn with oiled rod bent over his knee; came home with blue welts; from that hour unwilling to learn; marriage remains unseparated; united forever; the couple that has joined for eternity has unconsciously found the way to God's throne; three times need or death separate the marriage, more is punishable; three times separate the soul; in the beyond, blindness may fall from the eyes; believers are invited before His Allholiness throne; rejoined once more blessed; rejoice in your christendom; God's son has risen; sitteth to the right hand of his all-loved Father to judge the living and the dead. Spirit Elektro at your service in hell's chasm in the middle of earth."

Oskar Herzberg

OSKAR HERZBERG    Senile mania; excerpt from "The dragon, historical drama in 2 acts," exercise book with 39 sheets; and, texts (separately) for pictures, undated.

# GUSTAV SIEVERS†

UNTITLED

7.1.1919

With your permission!

The principal name among all barricades on earth is Turkey. Therefore, its regency also called itself the Porte,* because with this, the government wanted to show that it was through it alone that one could enter Heaven.

The things that differ greatly on Earth should also be the most isolated from each other. Thus, the Blacks and the Whites. The main task of this government was to guard the Dardanelles which represented the entrance to the <u>Black</u> Sea.

This entry way seems to have been the most vehemently disputed in the course of the past, but always held victoriously by Turkey. A key [*Kei*],** as it is pronounced, is of course a harbor installation and thus one sees that the whole name Turkey is fitting for this sea entry, and it takes a lot before anything on earth carries so much importance, that its right to the same should be recognized in such a main name, which encloses a large territory within itself.

However, the barricading of the Black Sea cannot apply to Africa's Blacks. It applies to the old world, inasmuch it is populated by Whites and they do not come into contact personally with Blacks at the places where they live. The fight for this Porte to the Black Sea demonstrates and best confirms the Negro world discovered by me in our zone. The danger of their detection here in our country was so great that the inhabitants were condemned to constantly eat black bread to mark an already existing togetherness with the Blacks. This worked even better here because an eater is also called a gnawer or rodent [*Nager*] and this is after all almost the same as Negro [*Neger*]. The

Germans already have Moorish villages in their moor bogs. The villages had to die out in these spots because there were open places there through which one could have invaded. But, because a village cannot be missing forever, the turf must represent the name of the village until it can come into existence again.

Just as almost everything inherently dangerous in the country can be traced back to the domination of a robber class, so also the moors. They were necessary because of these subjects who gave themselves the title of "Your Highness" and with these invaded the Negro world at these moor sites had they not educated themselves.

The danger lay mainly therein, that the Black Sea is a lake [See] and not an ocean. Thus it was called: the Black Sea [Schwarze See] and linguistically lacked only an N on the end of Sea [See], in order to make *the Blacks see [die Schwarze sehn]* out of that. Highnesses, who chased all women, would also have succeeded in this; they would have discovered the Blacks in this zone.

The existence of the mole demonstrates the effort with which evolution avoids Something like that. In this situation, the word nearer [naeher] would be linked first of all to sea [See], in order to make Lakes [Seen; Sehen - in original] out of it. This meant the discovery of the Negro world in our zone. But the devices of Nature are strong and in the name of the Blacks, which imposes itself, and which tritely means the same thing, seeing this more closely will be impossible, because nothing can be more contradictory than the black Negro. But not only with this alone is the path to the Blacks in our zone blocked, no, another individual, the mole, was created to prevent this. The question could arise, namely, what is a Negro? and the answer to that could be: If a Negro [Neger] is something comprehensible, then a gnawer*** [Nager] is certainly something that is better known and could very well be black and, that means, therefore: the black gnawers see. But that's wrong! This black gnawer is blind, and even though we can see him, he cannot see us and, thus, the seeing of Blacks in our zone is impossible, as long as they are members of a world of their own here; in that case they should be able to see as well.

Now please notice carefully that the mole never comes into daylight. He is born underneath our level, lives and dies under it, without having seen or walked upon it. In this way of life we are able to recognize a Negro world which exists with us at the same time in this zone.

Until now, it was never possible for one race to invade the world of another and only now, with my disclosure, can this be possible at a later date.

If you have doubts about these eminently scientific statements, that the mole is based on this link to the Black Sea and its entryway, the Dardanelles, I refer you to the names of the same. Look at the same time at the lips of the Negro, which protrude greatly and which are called raised: A mouth is also called a muzzle [Maul] and the muzzles [Maeuler] of the Negros are raised [aufgeworfen; Wurf, or Aufwurf, as noun] - a mole [Maulwurf].

Thus, the name came into existence because every Black is certainly a hunter but not a gnawer. As such, the Black throws a spear [Spehre, which is misspelled; the correct spelling is Speer], and only a muzzle can be opened wide [aufspaerren, which also is misspelled; correct spelling is aufsperren]. The similarity of the sounds of the words spear [Speer] and open [here, Spaerre, which actually means barrier] has combined in the name of this black gnawer the words muzzle [Maul] and throw [Wurf], because the Black, of course, throws with it.

This name construction, however, can be traced back essentially to the N that is missing from sea [See, i.e. Seen], because we often mistake these letters and this sea [See] in its designation as ocean [*Meer*] actually has such a letter that attracts the N in adjoining sea [*Nebenmeer*], since it actually is such a sea to which the mouth of the Dardanelles leads, which, as the most unusual of its kind, sanctions the name. If its mouth [*Mund*] has decided on muzzle [*Maul*], then the Dardanelles themselves have added the throw [*Wurf*], because throwing spears can just as well be called toss fast [*schnellen*] as throw [*werfen*] and even more so, because everything depends on how fast it happens.

To the ending of the Dardanelles [*Dardanellen*] the S from spears [*Speere*] itself is added, turning it into *Snellen,* just as the Sch from the color of the Negros [*Schwarz*] makes it into *Schnellen* [in English: toss fast].

This name of the link with the Mediterranean Sea also calls to mind the fast work of the mole. His raised hills represent the outlines of the Negros' dwellings. They rest on, for him, the eternally applicable label gnawer [*Nager*] and are mounds of soil [*Auf- oder Auswuerfe*], which are based on the A, with which he paraphrases his name as Negro.

These black gnawers [*Nager*] are those among the Whites, who counted themselves among the Highnesses, whose dangerousness I have already indicated.

I was able to identify with the utmost degree of certainty the dead mole, which I saw being buried in 1878 in a wood on the outskirts of Hanover by a swarm of gravediggers belonging to the insect world as the <u>soul of the last Hanoverian king</u>.

It is well known that King George V was blinded by a throw [*Wurf*]. This blinding of a Sovereign in just one eye leads one to the conclusion that the separation of the spheres is not to last much longer, that even with one eye one can still see enough. That is why these kings called themselves of the Guelphs [*von Welfen*]. That connects directly to the Blacks, who must be considered first to be seen.

Guelphs [*Welfen*] should mean world fairies [*Weltfeen*] and at the Black Sea wave fairies [*Wellfeen*]. The T in Turkey that cozies up to this ocean makes out of this clear designation only world fairies [*Weltfeen*]. The capital of the same demonstrates that the people there are by no means savages but are in a state of high civilization in which the nople [*nopel*] ending merely designates the noble.

Since this discovery I tremble before majesties and have also abandoned supporting this House in the recovery of Hanover. But this is all beside the point.

I don't believe in a Heaven the way the masses on earth imagine it to be. With this I want to say that there cannot be great differences in the spheres. I know Heaven very well. The Chinese, this mocked nation, inhabit it now completely by themselves. It is the Himalayas. The myth of heaven is based on it alone. We also speak thus of it in the name of this mountain.

All the world imagines it is possible only to set foot there with the permission of the eternal powers. Well, you see, it is walled in, cut off for every non-Chinese. The wall forms one of the Seven Wonders of the World. The Chinese must be the most peaceful people on earth. It has never gotten involved in world squabbles. Never has it demanded anything from others or threatened them with war. But all states want to harass it, right up to today.

The belief in a life in another and better world dates from the time when the parts of the world were not yet connected to each other, when they still did not know of each other.

But because the most unclean elements always force themselves as masters onto every faith, no one has thought in the least in discovering and getting to know each other, to announce the end of faith in another world, because now one finds it actually before one. And, in keeping with this, the discovery of America has turned the masses more joyfully to emigration rather than possibly inducing them to go to Heaven, because nobody has lungs strong enough to be a permanent singer of praises of that as prescribed by the clerics. It seems more agreeable to all to eat and drink well during that time.

The fact that the Porte also believed that it controlled Heaven arises from the symbol of the half-moon. However, I do not believe for a moment that it is barred to the Negros. I know of a nice city on the moon of about 50,000 inhabitants which is perhaps the most important of all. I have, however, only seen Whites on the same. I only mention this because, among those things which one believes about the height of Heaven, one could only understand the moon because it is considered part of the Earth and because on other world bodies their own populations need the space for themselves.

I do not think that the Porte was a reference to the Chinese Wall or that perhaps it could come under Turkish leadership to an invasion of Heaven, which I understand to be the Himalayas.

A people like the Chinese which is practically unarmed always endures the longest. The more arms, the closer the downfall. The Chinese will outlast us and everyone else. The name Turkey, meant to be a protection against spears,**** cannot be meant to blow up the visible heaven in China, to invade the Himalayas.

The names Turkey, Highness are inherently understandable, so that I did not believe it necessary to comment upon them. I also did not think it necessary to point out during the discourse itself that we calculate invisible events only on the basis of visible ones, which except for one letter mean the same thing, and which therefore permit definite conclusions based on themselves.

If you are interested in numerical proofs, be so kind as to support my lectures in that you expose my children's mean web of lies and assure me of a part of the interest from the considerable fortune left by my wife, so that I get the tobacco. I am also

burning with desire to get money for the small attempts*****
that should make it possible to keep on living. This will be hard
because in the name of my wife numbers have been spelled with
K which means, cannot, or rather, will not pay.

Yours respectfully,
Weber Sievers

TRANSLATOR'S NOTES:

†The author uses a great deal of wordplay. Key German words
have been included in brackets to make the context somewhat
clearer, at least for those readers with a basic knowledge of
German.
*Or, as used officially, the "Sublime Porte."
**Misspelled in the text: the correct German spelling for the
word is *Kai*.
***i.e., a rodent.
****Possibly spheres; the German word used is *Spaeren* which is
a misspelling, and which could mean either spears [*Speere*] or
spheres [*Sphaeren*].
*****Possibly: temptations; German word used is *Versuchen*,
which clearly is tests/trials, but he may have meant *Versuchungen*,
which is temptations; here, the small joys in life.

GUSTAV SIEVERS   Schizophrenic; 1919.


# JOHANNES FELIX ALEXANDER THEODOR TAUBER

Left and right turnaround writing these words! = amen pure
and all pure suns with all pure names and all sins = are, in 8

true creation mouths, written in themselves and all true creation mouths, are! Spirit, faithful true eternal, These words! = guilty spirits with all dirty names and all evil spirits with all = , are! in left and right turns written in themselves, in 8 left and right turnaround mouths of creation. These are also, True Mouths and are destruction mouths, that destroy forever all evil spirit, faithful, true,

Innocent souls in pain. These words! = afts* that a smallest part of the spirit of these, by all true gravities and by every movement, are one! written in left and right turnaround writing, 8 times in itself in true soul-mouths, with thought-connecting lines in reversing swords and safeties, side-links, connected.

The name Johannes, Tauber is! has been written in a breath-writing in fishbreathing writing with prism ray refraction. Johannes, Tauber drawn as breathing fish according to a breathing fish spirit. These breathing fishes have strengthened the ability to hear with every spirit and the face (to see the power of seeing in the truth). While listening-in on conversations and while looking (foreseeing and seeing the truth) one hears and sees. obediently Johannes, Tauber linked to the highest power of emotion.

The word obedient, must be pronounced correctly in the mental picture while listening. and must be presented mentally with correct pronunciation, this must occur as well during true see-ing, and also during prophetic seeing, here are some more good pointers while one has these mental pictures, as mentioned above, one pays attention to mouth movement, while listening in on conversations, while seeing one pays attention to the movement made by the people or the spirits one sees the true answer, while listening-in on conversations, one sees the true answer, in a mental picture and even hears it, Satan seeks to disturb the truth in these cases, and one is linked obediently, to Jahannes, signed Johannes, Felix, Alexander, Tauber, in every movmn = Theodor, Tauber. in Poehsnek in Thuer. (ingia) with the highest power of emotion. Residing, Brauhausgass 41.

TRANSLATOR'S NOTE:
*Apparently an invented nonsense word; German, *Aefte.*

JOHANNES FELIX ALEXANDER THEODOR TAUBER    Diagnosis (?); notebook with text and drawings, pen with black ink [title inscription by somebody else in yellow chalk], 1931.

## STEPHAN KLOJER

Dissipations, accountorization - concordation deed documentation; manuscription, rescription, contractualibity and contraction - the titulars of the adversations, monograms firms, inscriptions and superscriptions of the personal individual natural, figural, ornamental, signatural composed and published with the assistance of the most renowned autographs such as Bavaria. Karthaus Pruell the 25th of December 1895 Steph. Klojer.

Liturgical lexicon-reference, bulletin's, editorship plan speech literary tome-scribbling, breviary scribbling, project writing literary book production, seemingly "progr." typesetter's volume edition, note "prosp." printerly exercise book tab. of contents, account card "presserly brochure register coupon "Globus" newspaper editorship journal - ed. journal red. album scribbling alamanac writer annual - writ. protocol auth. etceteral table auth. bankruptcy.

As opposite and base of all creation, a six = to sevenfold fiscal, official, personnel and individual fed by the state coffers maintains its position and employment. Come down from higher schools and seminarist unions and worlds I lack very frequently all decent writing and language, rhetoric and eloquence. Officially and authorized, privately and well as civilly personally and individually I assumed indeed these sympathetic exemplary addresses and titles which are connected with Stephan Klojer only since August 18, 1895. Since that time I remain according to plan and project from imaginary Klojer Weber families general descendant relationship a. born and descended from dukedom Schwand Glassra Heinxdorf, and I function in the state coffers' - operated medical medicinal hospically lazaretish and corpse-autopsyish fools deranged imbecile sanatorium Karth. fool maniac raving-Institute Pruell. Generally and completely suffering all disease epidemics plague systems painfully considered and subjected to I am since the 14th year of the adressatic assumption of the economic from idustrial agricultural manufactural official service as well as private civilistic home farm and property personally prevailed I see myself corporeally and bodily sensually uningeniously reduced and run down. I have to regard myself, to wit, as an unnatural phenomenon and little virtuoso and ma[. . .], and don't enjoy anymore since the end of May of last year any of my numerous economic agricultural, as well as industrial and manufactural 666.-777 family ties any more. Newspaper deadline February 29, 1896. Klojer Stephan, Schultor* of the Gro Romo Rahmo.

TRANSLATOR'S NOTE:
*Schultor* is normally a school gate, but probably a nonsense word here.

STEPHAN KLOJER    Dementia praecox; excercise book with text and drawings, 1895/96.

# JOSEPH SCHNELLER

V.k.H.
Clergymen are hell-
scientists fleshdevouring-
guilt, which even the lamb of god
won't take away the sins of the
world and which innocence helps as
much as the doves, which in the end
serve only as sacrifice for God.
God is Cott = feces = earth*
Eternal life = Ah-weigh,** i.e. that
life is weighed anyway.
If one hadn't learned a language,
one wouldn't know about a
religion.
The World-Nature-Ladder-
    Level.

SOMETHING MODERN.MOLDS and SOMETHING
MOLDERED.MOLDERING.***

TRANSLATOR'S NOTES:
Three German plays on word transformations:
*Gott = Cott = Kot = Erde
**Gott ist ewig (i.e. God is eternal = Eh-wieg)
***MODERNES.MODERD u. MODERNDES. MODERND.

JOSEPH SCHNELLER (pseudonym: Sell)   Schizophrenic; 1920.

The spiritual activity pursues with its energy dimensionally and in certain velate proportions the regression and the progression, which give rise to its external effects. It is these dimensionary bases that the soul ascribes, with recognition of doubleactivity affects understood or not, in a first totality of establishing such resulting purpose to outside influence. All feelings of pleasure and all feelings of grief ascend a scale, which, though, it exists in a gradation distinct from internal affect, really runs parallel to it, creating a criterium between the relation to the monads of the outside world and one's own pearly impulses. If we initiate the excitation of this inclination, for example, by reading a poem for the love of poetry, we base the practice on the clarity of consciousness, even though the impulses of love for pure poetry would occur later, inasmuch as we are dealing with monads whose feeling and hoping could not be expressed clearly, whose love would exist unconsciously before the experience of reading, and whose aversion would want to be cancelled out by heightened interest - in other words, we do not abandon the psychology of the soul's anticipation. Furthermore, we would have to deal with the restruction of the diet, which dimensionally causes the unopposed repulsion of part of all other activities of the soul. In this, self-preservation should be practiced and cultivated in all walks of life. The body is strengthened. The soul also must be strengthened by wise schooling in the beautiful, the true and the good, and the recognition of the efforts towards that end. We base our theme on the last point of view of the recognition of efforts in which the dimensionary preceding determinations are easy and especially since this point of view first of all, seems to be ripe and, secondly, very well suited for our purpose, to demonstrate the higher love of the monads. Therefore, we read, and after such a dissection for the dimension of the theme, it is just as easy to take into account the dimensionary recognition as it is psychologically easy to recognize the sequence.

MORITZ WEIL    Manic-depressive; letter with drawing (double sheet), 1900.


## HYACINTH BARON VON WIESER

Dear Father!

The way the family is neglecting me is somewhat painful. Today I had again several ideas which bring me to the point that I would like to continue to work with you on your astronomical book. Unfortunately, my beginnings in physics are too slightly developed, and I have no way to obtain the means for that. I sit all day and calculate (also during the night) the possibilities of how the astronomical, the proper method of mathematics can be led via biology to sociology. I'd like very much to travel. I am incarcerated, and human reason which says that on occasion one must be outside in the free world, unfortunately is not there. Limp and in a bad mood, I get a bad reputation among the people around me, though I am really happy when I am working. And I work all the time. I tell you, father, I'll still solve the problem of life. Because the following sequence is already as clear as the sun:

(maybe you will think a bit further, as I do, about these mutual thoughts.)

Astronomy: the science of the united bodily forces, of the stars for <u>hundreds</u> of occurrences. The metrict system; the beginning of the rational world view.

Physics: the science of the movement of bodies by <u>forces</u>.
(Forcology)

Chemistry: (Materiology)

Radiology: (Material radiation)

Biology: Beings 8 deltoid

Psychology:

Sociology:

Unity

---

Beings which live on each other and in each other, Un-good ones
Only totally separate personalities can complete a journey
through the world
<u>I</u> am the most personal that can possibly exist in the world.
(definition of "I")

Ha, you, hahahahahahaha!
(purepana) nananananananana!
Into the breakdown!
If you have 7, order, cleanliness,
heaviness, luck, occupation,
life (song!), love
If you have those 7
Hahahahaha.

The man

<u>Willology</u> is the idea of the soul in nature.

Chapter
1 A lively contemplation of the science of the will.
2 The correct judgment of the process of willing
  guidepost, safeguard

3 the highest life form (man) is the <u>clock-hand of</u> nature
4 Rhythm (Ur, Uhr (clock*) ouren
5 God's peace (Trenga dei, Olympia, the golden age)
6 Glimpses (origin of life)
  (link to radiology)
  Gas
7 ~~Air~~ crystals birds, easy movability,   Nothingness
8 Star matter, stars' influence, world form      lid

                              content, wisdom
                              vessel
9 Species/sexes,** the concept of species/sex, the sexual act
  (maleness)
10 Amiabilty, the directions of the curves, will transfer, swings,
  positivsm

  connection with
                              yes
language (soc.) (zillions)
                              direction
Advertisements (market)
                              e.g. normality
Numbers (makes)
                          progress
                          straps (   )
                          eyepoints
Triple number      Ostbohrer Castle
          [. . .]
          colors in the rainbow spectrum

$=$ chemical wave fronts
definition of light (compare riddlelogy: love)
influencing the will
magic (historical)

TRANSLATOR'S NOTES:
*A play on words - ur (like ur-instinct; the same meaning in English and German), *Uhr* is German for clock/watch. *Ouren* is unknown.
**The word *Gescnlecht* means both "sex" and "species," also race, stock, lineage, extraction, family.

---

1. Full-of-life contemplation of the science of the will (not volition)*
   a. It is a fact that the will occurs in nature, in biology and in man.
   b. The will is that which overcomes the friction of the clarities.
   c. The clarities maintain quite definite directions whose crossing is strenuous.        (auto-motor organisms)
   d. the conditions of will occur especially with stars, self-propelling organisms (heart activity?), flying machines (because they cannot obey man absolutely), in gas clouds/vapors.
   e. With another pre-occupation, the trajectory changes.
   f. It is laws, that guide the will.
   g. The will is the concentration of the entire space motion, the maleness, the me (I-sensation, I-sense). It is the phenomenon of the center of gravity that guides it. It is sufficient unto itself.

Correct judgment of the process of the will.

   a. Life is a thing unto itself. The dream of my creation moves through the world. to walk is somewhat more abstract than

Life. To keep relatively quiet, to move forwards, to jump (with women, to step back, children's movements, men ref. morality, sociology 1). are manifestations of externally visible demonstration of the will. We assume that.

b. Above and beyond the essence of the will, man can hardly intrude into nature. Children and women often have deeper views that can destroy the male (e.g. Nietzsche). Obviously the concept of philosophy is thus denied (ref. morality)

To counteract airplane sickness, 1 somersault to the east on a blue sofa.

We view in advance the nervous element of the following parts as gifted with will: right toenails, right knee (both whole), male erogenous zone, right** hip, teeth (clenching), chin (difference to animals is most obvious, also interesting in racial terms), beard, right eye, female thought of the male, brain right top backwards edge of the head.

The easier the mobility, the clearer the will has to be. Tiny gas bubbles wherever, certainly can be looked at societologically. Science, unfortunately, has not been able to indentify gas crystals, which should be located nearby due to rapid adaptation of the life process. Birds' will(s) operates by the rapidity of the eyes.

TRANSLATOR'S NOTES:
*Author makes distinction between words *Wille* and *Willen*, which doesn't seem to exist, at least not according to dictionary.
**Probably a misspelling in the text, which in the original reads *echte* (i.e. genuine) rather than *rechte* (right) hip.

<u>Normal daily schedule.</u>
The forgotten is not defenseless!

6  One has to know when one got up.
Regularly get up (7 a.m.!)
(right or left leg normal swing)
Get up, immediately out of bed. Numbers: recite briefly
main goal,* walk daily number of steps, <u>10 exercises make
exercise numbers</u>, call, bring to mind mantic** numbers.
touch triple flash with 1.
7  Put on suit coat. Form nerve barometer numbers, read aloud
morning lines,
ten times quietly, only write down evening lines.
Call out: three times blaha 10 left swinging with the head;
drawing 10 circles, 10 winks, 10 noseups, 10 points
with the nose on the wall, exclaim marriages.
1 R (3 lengthistics 5.8.)

Springoutwardsillion!
Left-right (10)calm. <u>Indispendsable: Zenithlook, Sirius. Left,
exaggeration. Stretch. I blackhead</u>(left hand), <u>10 exercises</u> 10
number, 3 friends, <u>inspiration for oneself</u>, small jump.

variously. Vocal exercises: (10 Rim) + 1) 10 + equalization
+ Vienna whistling; Runschaken rem-
matschakerlfaualya;#
Blowcall: (a aha yeah, lat jalldalailamal bat jal
fart harsch tat hahala yeah hat.# (10 + 1), say after
ten: Art, bricklayer piano, ten, finally slasitendi
artakal#

Mirror blood. Harteknar hartlestalmanalhat;# "I am a man:"
say <u>Lim Rim Himalaya</u>. Left corner of the mouth:
cheerfulness.

Washing: Eau de Portugal left temple, armpits, chest 3 clocks
(heart, star, will); face upwards (moon, nose S,
eyes left 10, right 10 + 10, forehead 19, cheeks 6,
ears 4, chin 7 head back.
start wash with right hand only, grab soap with left,
neck
no magic seeing,*** grab toothbrush with left, (5.
exactology will). Is good to use mouth cloth. + =
Kalodent.****
Matter stroke right 10 times, 3 rings, little finger.
Practice poses. Brush (across): earth flash, sun
apex (parting of hair)***** 29 times, Vega orbit 8
times; beard clockwise from outside; metal comb is
good.

Dressing (towards north, throw on shirt, right hand
first), Julreif:#
perhaps Ahaha hat, ert, or Hall, wit witwitenozeler
char. or, har, har namferdur# (primebloomspringoutward-
sillion) dress in parallel; first right, then left,
don't reach across to other side; don't reach into
pockets; grab star strokes on left; 3 nonsenses (has)
speak to a firmplace during tie knotting; Eau
de Col. 3 handkerchiefs and hand, 3 finger pull (left
to right, right twice);
49 little hops circle left. poke
towards east at the wall (vegastinic)
8 Hand practise 42 glasses of water. Belt grip
9                write books for 3 hours, if possible outside
                    Predict occult with pencil, short-

hand, speak loudly, call out, howl
To see men (not society types or
women) is good
especially during forenoon.

10 H Nullus dies sine linea correcta.
Lecture preferably 12-1. (In the
morning it shouldn't be after 8.)

11 Stone ax circle, 5 tongue-lickers (3 above, 2 below, clockwise)
left

12 12.10 toilet (seasoning, perfumed (some Eau de Portugal)
paper.)
10' sleep (blue sofa if possible)
19 eye exercises: frog stare, rider stare (towards east if
possible),
point stare (to a solar); chimneysweep stare
(13 times . . .), clamp stare
17 times left, 19 times right, staff stare 21 times,
right stare (left-right 10times, 25 times);
3 corner, 4 corner, 5 corner (each 10 times,
preferably something hanging);

13 eye roll (stop on the right, roll left),
in-the-lead stare (to right) fast sense, slow
will. Light in a slit (always view slits,
holes, dark things left below).
Hyperbolstare. Assessing stare. Whale stare. 10erstare
(Look at 10 nice things for a long time). Dimensions
stare (Point-emotion-music of the spheres). Take golden
things. Open eyes, shut, open).

While going to dinner, 10 times towards north: metric
measuring system keep Jews to left (announce Dar, Har,
gar)******
Eat soup in silence. Blow over the food. Dear little right

finger plays at tasting. Salad with fingers!
Don't look at the bottom of the spoon. Sit
towards the right (don't cross left foot)
14 After dinner: 10 H, 13.14 h sleep or less later.
Push-ups 10 times.
Sofa. prone exercises.     (See morality in picture).
15 Drink water. (2½ liters every day, not during meal).
Instinctual
ideas are good.

No more poems if there's a lecture
15.45 Look at the sun, through telegraph wires wherever
possible. or the sky.
16

Soil in left hand. (June-July solstice any finger into
the ground.)
e.g.          Limrimhimalaya 10 (chestnuts)
17 10      1 hour sports: running (at least 1 km, 10 numbered
with E[. . .], and count), be exhausted, eye
exercises (1-3 leg exercises, bowling balls, 3 color
comparison, count 10 colors, sky, women,
telegraph wires), watch flying things, lie on earth
(place stones or similar, [. . .] kinds of various
things (imagine light meridian), 10 jumps
eastward,
demonstrations (100 times) fencing exercises air swings
(at least 10 times)
Don't take notice of women, flowers, religion during the
exercise.
17.30 Sleep for 1 second [. . .]

Afternoon hour: 17.30-18.30. make a little poem (perhaps
18          from morning). Enjoy colors, count same,
paint, draw with left hand, make music, compose

19  10 H Supplement by R wherever (this non-movement no more
         after supper)-place tongue on left outside of teeth(at
             least every 7th day Monday is best!)
     19h22'45″ Love hour (never past 22h): The mouth is wiped.
         (During a love night (better evenings) coitus
         should be before 24h).
20  After supper: future ideas, thoughts of god, droll story.
    Be sociable in evenings!
21
    Whenever possible, go to bed at 22h. (bed in northerly
    direction, head better toward the east). No chamberpot in
    the room!
    Eye exercises before falling asleep: 3 blue, red like blue,
    any colors, color bands, picture, new thing
    bodily), glossy colors, bright spots, distance
22  Rest towards southeast. estimate, star (or weather) glimpse,
    10 glimpses through the room (left, right above).
    10: guess, wish, evaluate to northwest. millering-in
    (leg circling once left, 10 times right towards east). Leg
    swinging (Kurt). Left a little. Leg back.
23  Night hand washing, possibly arm movements (clamly)
    Staxeln (*******) (Day number). Jump into bed. Roll
    up inside blanket from north west. Boldly fall asleep
    (80 ways). Don't think about women.
24  (eyes closed). Noble early rise.          Sirius. Don't touch
                                              prick. Calculate.
1                                             No star love.
    Day's end.                                Left hand sideways.
                                              rectum
2                                             left ass cheek.
3
4
    = night's end.

The early bird gets the worm.\*\*\*\*\*\*\*\*

TRANSLATOR'S NOTES:
*May be misspelling: German reads *ziel*, i.e. goal; but in the numbers context, writer may have meant *haupt zahl*, i.e. cardinal numbers.
**Noun *mantik*, the art of occult prediction.
***Uncertain; apparently a verb construction from the archaic.
****Presumably a brand of toothpaste of the period.
*****Play on words: *scheitel* means both part of the hair as well as apex/summit/peak.
******Uncertain; German text has question mark after the word; possibly a reference to some sort of exercises before going to bed.
*******Uncertain.
********English equivalent to German proverb which literally translates as "the early hour has gold in its mouth."
#Meaningless nonsense word.

HYACINTH BARON VON WIESER (pseudonym: Welz)  Schizophrenic; 1912.


# CARL LANGE

Cristo viene, los muertos se levantan!
"Christ is coming, the dead are arising."

is written at the source of a crime kept secret for 15 years by impudent, knowing falsification of documents by methodically crazy poison murderers and killers in Germany, that began with a judicial murder stigmatized by a habeas corpus order instigated by mentally deranged doctors in the service of American railway subsidy-swindlers in Mexico and that ends with a miracle of the Holy Spirit, as shown in the accompanying drawing,* a miracle in the shoe slip sole insert of the ruthlessly sacrificed, legally incapacitated, declared-as-dead victim of secret, brutal poisoning and crushing of the brain by satanically-obsessed, mentally deranged assassins. A four-page picture inside the sole of a shoe in connection with a new secret poison double murder which is understandable and interpretable only on the basis of the photographs of my deceased parents Eduard and Mathilde Lange, nee Conrad, and their nine children. The parents, of which the father, deceased in 1893, was brutally, crudely cheated without his knowledge, was betrayed in a manner that exposed the entire German civil service while my mother was overtaken by death ten years earlier in 1883, unmask in this wonderful picture, seemingly inexplicable to everybody as well as myself, the cursed murderers of their son under the sign of the holy ghost, a white dove and the sign of affliction, a black cross that depicts the secret shattering of brain and backbone, the crucifixion of the head, which with loss of beard, hair and eyebrows, facial scars and spots has buried unmistakable marks of the hidden crime, while mother throws down the gauntlet with her hair, wound with a hairband into an idiomatic picture and pinned up with combs, demanding revenge "hair for a hair." For more details, see Extra edition. Carl Lange.

TRANSLATOR'S NOTE:
*The drawing is not reproduced in the anthology.

CARL LANGE    Schizophrenic; separate text with drawing, undated.

# MAX JUNGE

MICROCOSMIC THOUGHT PRESENTATION BY M.J.R.
THE ALPHABETIC CHARACTER
THE CENTRAL POINT

Max Jung
To the directorate of the Provincial Insane Asylum in the City of
Leubus aO
attention asylum director public health officer Mr. Dr. Dinter,
Cloister Leubus aO
Due to urgent necessity of the purely thinking and affirmative
matter, to be represented by M.J.R. in the interest of all science
everywhere, and here by the psychiatrist as THE PERSON IN
SILENCE, I, due to the need for something singular and a
compelling requirement for my own work, am forced to ask here
most politely whether I may take 1 sheet of writing paper as well
as 1 envelope of my choice from the stock of writing materials of
the asylum here, and whether, according to a directive yet to be
issued by the acting asylum head physician Mr. Dr. Fuenfstueck,
will actually be permitted to be handed such. So far as all these
permissions, sought in this matter by means of these LINES OF
WRITING, can be granted, I also ask most kindly at the same time
to return this sheet of PAPER, specially technically prepared by
M.J.R.
City of Leubus aO M. Junge
On March 10 1918
In order to facilitate psychiatric studies on the living, the corres-
ponding NOTE OF APPROVAL is requested HEREUNDER.
IN NOTHING read and APPROVED
S
Director of the Prov. Insane Asylum, City of Leubus

<u>EVERYTHING</u> read and <u>PERMITTED</u>

x

Acting head physician of the Provincial Insane Asylum, City of Leubus aO

Dr Fuenfstueck

MAX JUNGE    Schizophrenic; drawing and text on both sides, 1918.


## MARIE-LOUISE M.

## LAST WILL AND TESTAMENT

I don't want anything more passionately than
not to be buried
in this room!
Because first of all
I just don't care if in this
    room
the piano is removed
    and my
    mother's
    children's coffin
    is put here
2ndly 1.2 it's repulsive that
my napkins are to be counted.
    III I don't want any
    deaconess near my
    bedstead
and 4th
    4. commandment

I will permit myself
to believe in the
transmigration of souls.
Ulli Feuerlaender also Louis Kaatz
    senior
    can go to
    Haiti
and intone the
    eternal melody

MARIE-LOUISE M.   Manic-depressive; double page with text and
drawings, undated.

## ELISE MAHLER

Tit city councillor
threat of war to my bosses who have me in prison many years
already, family notice Elise Mahler Susanna ditto Mrs. Widmer
Maler "nephew" Grambach Gottfried Ulrich Paris Heinrich
Hans Alfred Rudolf and the devil's parents Rudi Mahler and
Marg. Trachsler my murderers torturers and rogues
The world is full of devilish people, 6 brothers never had any
brains, reason only tormenting all day and night all with women
and children These 10 brothers and sisters have abandoned me
and treated me impudently sharply and robbed me and the
friends have helped in the crime

Murder asylum!!!
Tit asylum administration
It can't go on like this with the persons. with their ordering about
all the people, be it at table with the food, which is served almost

like to the pigs and that the people eat their fill for the ridicule of the women guards. These women guards only want to dress neatly and beautifully so they look beautiful before the gentlemen, but would give the people the most horrid food, if you could only be here, there are even sick women here who never wash their mouth, and they then often smear about the food spoons and bowls, and such sick ones should make me sick throw up, what I have seen sometimes, that the women guards take nauseous food and give it to others and the horrible ladles and forks are not healthy.

Demand release My son demand from this murderer's hut

ELISE MAHLER    Diagnosis (?); undated.

## AUGUST KLETT

Royal Sanatorium Weinsberg Feb. 5, 1909

Dear Aunt Luise,

I wrote to dear Mama yesterday and come to you today to thank you so much for your water* and cookies for Christmas. Uncle Fritz in an oval picture - of negative imagination, I saw him yesterday without hat cigar in his mouth turning it with his right hand, going from west to east, the eyes fixed to the ground. The snow screen - Prof. Lang high school Heilbronn illustrated lecture business association - has already taken the long way into the center of the earth, where our deceased in our cemeteries rushing with their bodies to the kernel of the walnut with milk-and-honey lives, waiting to return in the spring blossoms with flour and egg and fish, in water and spirit "because otherwise you can't come into the kingdom of heaven," asks our Lord Jesus Christ. The snow as corpse juice of the human body, which turns the animal world to gold, has in its flesh and deathlife the nature (or the "tara" in other words the cornea of the apple-of-the-eye earth (whose gross weight slumbers in the center) and outside on the annual average 20 degree heat according to Celsius at 144 kilometers daily ride over 365 days equals 52'560,000 kilometers path length, a total of 1051'200,000 kilometer-degree heat in its manifestations as moonlight, sunlight and astral (Aeronal = tomato = water pollen = cold blood = magnetic iron (copper = iron: cow, horse, bird, warm blood) the wrong oath in its word, is as phosphorus the "glow worm" its tickle and burn (cold burn and light) the sore throat (glitter Hamburg, Zeileck Frankfurt/ Main (Owl-tick), the whooping cough, influenza and grippe (1), means the superbillion of the number or salt crystals of the sheepwoolnerves or lightveins (Glauber's salts alkaline) Radatta =• R. ★= riding school the riding earth hours as race horse with valkyrie cloud figures, onward to God to Valhalla near "Regensburg" and is called tartrate of wine "saliva = spittle = Venacetin, corpse juice = cothurnus** = whore feces = water glass Meissner Heilbronn). Antipyrin is probably the same as this potassium namely burr oil in the resurrection out of the eye mirror, the songs of the golden earth (aurum = ear = conch) the molecules as proof of nature 1/5th cubic of a centimeter of life is worth 0.6 pfennig gold currency according to Lord Mayor Hegelmeyer it is just

insofar the same on that same accepts
a half Thaler's worth = of human semen whored into the air.
    A Heilbronn snowflake.
    diamonds = earth star.
    Heart = Ores***
    Blackheart = Tar lava (Lavater)***
    Clover leaf = (Clover head = Klett)***
        Sugar blue = Glass

21. January whalebone, Feb. wool, March cattle hair, April fish
scales, May snake skin; June rabbit hair, July bird feathers,
August game hair, Sept. bristles, Oct. cranium, Nov. horse hair,
Dec. women's hair, Dec. Jan. 21 men's hair. - as crystals of the
animals' bodies (eagles) our blood ores - are supposed to clothe,
feed, illuminate humanity and the morning of the pupils' blue
life, the diorama of the stimulus life of the rings at noon, holiness
and rotational power of salvation in the evening and this flake
tear of the myrths**** in the emotional life of the myrths in the
ascent and decline in the Orient (humans, of the latrine (declin-
ascendents in tar white = wheat grain) they should greet them,
(rain) as I greet you. Your grateful nephew

August Klett

TRANSLATOR'S NOTES:
*Possibly a shortened reference to Eau de Cologne (in German,
*Koelnisch Wasser*, Cologne Water).
**A play on words; in German original, *cothurn = hurenkot*: in
a tragic/majestic/pompous style = whore feces.
***Alliterative plays on words: *Herz = Erze, Schwarzherz =
Teerlava*, (Lavater), the latter is apparently a nonsense word;
*Kleeblatt* (clover leaf) = *Kleekopf* = Klett, the patient author's
last name.
****Possibly an invented word, a combination of "myrtle" or
"myrrh" and "myth" - the word similar in German and English.

---

:Seadear - in a grey
downy felt hat youth sleeps
stretched out = she doesnt
knit any more: 40000
francs you lost tonight = Kuebler

tapped a barrel, filled with
ice, that straw became
expensive, and they asked
for drinks = the rats gnaw on the
toes, the murderer climbs
out of the coffee: "come along, Maire-
to the main police station:" there
are still prisoners coming:"
> But you shouldn't do that,
> > to push the <u>Pomeranian into</u>
> > <u>the Mannheimer's jaws</u>
> > > a) <u>push out picture of Luise Ruedenauer, H.</u>
> > <u>Trost, the</u>
> > > b) <u>dog thoughts</u> (4)
> > could bite off your
> > > <u>Cinius</u>10 (27) (9)
> > thing.

"Just think, Mrs. <u>Lifeinsuranceinspector,</u> - my Persian servant just told me - that rundown <u>Donna Theresa</u> von Schoerner supposedly maintained a Turkish Mephisto behind <u>the scenes</u> - to dry her <u>nose</u> and to bite off her admirers

"My mother as a girl."
"Keep in mind that your mother also was a girl once;" the lady from Savoy (7) of the <u>"Province of Belgium"</u> (6). The <u>spirit</u> gave her <u>strength</u> and <u>justice</u> and she learned <u>discretion</u> at the fountain of <u>wisdom</u> = <u>bird, knight and bull</u>: the <u>tinsel charm</u> was born, from the <u>magical spring</u> of <u>the winged bottlery</u>: the <u>stork</u> helped her toward <u>greatness</u> and the <u>questing zenith</u> to <u>tight-ness</u> = she was = never at the <u>lever of the grinding ornament</u>: a <u>whetstone spark</u> for the <u>milk jet</u> of <u>steel</u>: the <u>ear cipher</u> of the strange was her <u>German way</u> of the "<u>frogneedlelizard-agility</u> =

when crocheting the contracts about felteggcloths of the wind-
ings: something lasting and durable in plant shadow and cellar
plant of the picket-stockade-ray-sun over walls and vexations of
the state's flashiness
Weinsberg, 14-7-1915- v. Klett

---

TRANSLATOR'S NOTE: The following consists of two free-verse
poems, written on alternate lines.

## BAKING OVER HEAT AND ICE-COLDNESS
Weinsberg, July 13 1915
v. Klett

The white stockings are black, Stibbe =
in the yeasty wreath cake of the hottest urges stands
    (7, 1, 12, 6, 5, 2, 3, 4, 5, 6, 8, 3, 13, 11, 12, "97 = 7)
behind the bottom shape a baker and a
    a) Sister G. Hagenbucher-Joh. Schoellkopf (= -)
priest = love is red = and a
    1(x) to "you were at the belt" - to Schoeneck 1876 M 10.-?
lady fell victim to the same
    to a)"Before you bathe in the Neckar, you clean the teacher's
    feet
from heartsblood = she still says a prayer
    to b) We saw, with Uncle Fritz, nothing white on the lady?
for a dish of lentils in the hands of slumber
    Why do they frantically delay separation from the mother =
Mayer is gutsy: how do you know that.
    "The guys can't stand you talking to your friends."
pale brat chills the feet of both
    Why exactly was it Schneider-Stopf-Rueckert?
nostrilmen, because the ice bird

:"The others are the bychetes,* these coneubes* ( = &)
cools the pastry mightily with water acid
   There is somebody looking for an American: Chicago 1893
      Schmidt
while the foliage oven of the rope's decay
still swallows like a goose that just eaten goldfish-corn, and
   suddenly cackles all languages at
once in rabbit quack quack = then you present the mountain-
top-stick in vain, have burned the hat
for nothing, in the bread parlor of the water = and fire =
samples.

Doveswallowsyellowfreemasonbuildingart
Mortarfirshspiritlimefeet are the bootmakers

TRANSLATOR'S NOTE:
*Adaption of German words *Bycheten* and *Coneuben* in original. Dictionary does not list them, and German-only dictionary
has no entry for them.


## WAELSUNG: EVII WM

England France
Weinsberg 2.11. 1912

The "Kavallo" lett K a Valois: in other words, August Valois is
the name of the new firm:
Wallhardt Interlacken - Wallraf
Richardsmuseum Cologne Rhine
Liege (Verviers) Namuri: zero Belgian, (French) Italy are there
("fib")
(21) (3)
The whole-oil of Aquarius in the January of the sciences, con-
noisseur: moonelies.

The zero or Madame Luna indicates a lady in blue on the floor, a black dog in the white fork of the pants, a universal dog on the left, whose genitals she plays with, while the other licks like all get out: Friedrich) Glaser should examine that fishy character, before entering the athletics club, "you are bastard pig, the honor is mine, says Dr. Sailer, it's supposed to have happened that he fucked somebody in the ass, named Supp: on the right a brother, during the act "rocking by himself" the other one she is supposed to have loved with even more horniness: it is supposedly the skyturning, the tossed bosom, the upper and lower, letting father and brother do it to her at the same time, even while standing on her head, "Beutelspach, is supposedly the emperor's seat and the castle about 4 million marks to build frisky

and that's supposedly known in Wuerttemberg, that he is strongly romanesque, in the state office.

Mr. Keller moved to M7, because they appreciate him there in France, but here in Italy (with Bulgaria) on the other hand Mr. Lutz moved in M1

we are informed that Skutari has not yet fallen, the "Besemen"* push together and the march to Constaninople is well on its way over "dirt holes": the little musical clock for 18$\underline{M}$ bought during its time from Nagel, by the imperial ottoman court purveyor, doesn't mean my mother's salon, there are also "needles" in it,

from Cramer Klett Needle Factory A.G., Bavarian Imperial Count Nueremberg, does one rechristen the lord mayors Bohnenmueller + Buns-Hofheimer-Ferguson Apolda - would have stood in silence with someone called Fuchs without a china chest in silence: the apple farmer supposedly happened on the scene with the "hornisgrinde"**: the ladies' pants sizer:

the "real mess," the doctors' tothehighheavenstink, and the scramble over roots and rocks, probably into the hole from the same, is supposedly mr. director's honor: he supposedly slept that

night in Japan as well, where they screwed him over\*\*\*: the scar
"777" triplestrawberryblossomperfume we smelled in the
stenchdefense: the giddy characters guys farted, shat whored
through the night: he "is okay byme" - dog must be beaten: he
doesn't like it at all.

TRANSLATOR'S NOTES:
\*and \*\*: No entries found for these words in dictionary.
\*\*\*German word is *vernardenkoettern* which is not in dictionary. This is an instinctive approximation at best.

---

"Don't be so coarse, Your Majesty, German Emperor and King
of Prussia, Wilhelm by the Grace of God, I don't want to give
you a well as a present.

The country priest to tollhatthumbscrewsetter D412 and: navy-
head - priestcatspawrippernumsculldumplingring - biter biter-
Launer-Noller-Pressel-Seeber Roller stomachdoormansspleen-
larynxgompera privy councillor Dr. Wackes-Klink to stomach-
doormanslit bib dop-ffel" Hacker-Kluss file to Victor file Rein-
frank-Fleischmann-Krauss = Schaefer Schieferer-Noerwaag
Waerter Kohlberger.

How does the tapewormeye vanish at the nervebandribstring It
is an achievement of the twofold circlecavalry = and owns a
lampwhip of the gold of gasolinechalk: "Ligroine"

Polygon point = on the whale, the laurelman rides with pleasure into the barrel-Rooster under the boneneckring of the
stingass-holehat from fishergame of the salad-
    to Donant-Decker: I am neither forester nor hunter
bible screwing: steel, a little push, the Count Strauss of Tolstoi
Lodge-" Gold (94)

(O) (4)
18 glass feathers = 18 basement moons
        c) Tone rods = flute, clarinet, piccolo, fife etc
have lost their shine = supply replacements-
the ray-stung aft-eye with which
        d) Madame-Miss Rosalie Mayer-Blaess
centrallensbulletshot of the tonguetesticles
                = rose children's league (O)
nerverootends fartlet in an arc

---

The opposite of the Antichrist, not in the ominous allembracing word "filth" but in the pure revelation by the light-angle of the room, consisting of glass and crosses, with its bowls of hail on sun rays and cloud bursts, while and colored lights, in the face of the vulgar in clouds of water vapor and earth hills in the splendor of the January light, the February jest, the March snow, the April storm, the May thaw, the June bloom, the July miracle, the August power, the September glow, the October fruit, the November ice, the Dezember honor, should take place over the glittering tones of the flowers and the blossom-metal-glory in their green undergarments and life'sdeath in the grain of seed. The trees (Bohemia), die corals (Orange), angels (Birds) England, crustaceans (Australia) asses (Asia) shopkeepers (America) cattle (Europe - cow) coffee plants (Africa) offer for spring's resurrection anew for beautiful Italy guide-harm = savior*, to the right the murderer Adria-Darius = King of the Persians = swineherd as a Serbian, to the left the Thyrrenian (murderer) the horrified herd, above their heads the old man (Aetna) on Sicily, the silent ash of belief with his tricky** son, Vesuvius, in the mountain lakes of the Alps and the Appenines the 30 pieces of silver, silver lakes, the silver in the moon, the gold in the sun, in the stars myrrh incense in the air the incense of the world and time, the open and closed space, of the Maurus (January 15), and Aries, Cancer and Libra, Capricorn will delight and enchant the month, the nomad as lady of fashion*** with the newest to the oldest of the great all-mother of total humanity and without sin in the animal world, the angel Eval, the gospel in color tones and music, air, light, water, (R) plants, humans, sky. The coat for which the dice were tossed, Marocos, is admired in astonishment by the Savior's mother, by the Indian (woman) Armenia, and Josef's wisdom sparkles in Sofia.

TRANSLATOR'S NOTES:
*Virtually untranslatable alliteration; in German: *Leit-Leid = Heiland.*
**Apparently invented word, "Pfipf," possible link to *pfiffig,* (smart, tricky).
***Play on words: in German: *Mode Dame.*

AUGUST KLETT (pseudonym: Klotz) Schizophrenic; excerpts, 1906, 1914, 1915, 1919, 1921.

## RUDOLF HEINRICHSHOFEN

10-18 1895. State's attorney v. Buttler 1. very excited. "A man who knew only princes, how did you get here again, what kind of crime is this again?" Scandalous "rape of a human being." Court Secretary Werthaeuser, of Gotha.

10-20 1895 Dr. Busch brought a letter. "Your wish has now been granted, you are in a state institution." Busch laughed colossally, yells, "the comedy of errors." 4000 jews, jew count Count Bernsdorf 11-6, 1895. "Come into my arms my son, in Berlin you're out with the empress, you must get away with the queen of heaven." etc. In February Heller came, everybody happily moved, but also dismayed. He stayed for 6 weeks in bed, in which a large knife was found on one occasion, he was supposed to have attempted suicide. He always nodded to me from the window with a laugh. After 6 weeks he got up, went with us Sundays down to the villa, when three gentlemen arrived in haste, hymn-books under their arms, stopped him "Heller, Heller, Heller." I had already reached the Goetting brickyard when Buttler came rushing after me "If you run away now, they'll get you back."

Vienna 1896. The three men stood kind of fearfully in a corner. I asked therefore, "What's the matter with them?" "Well, they're going into the madhouse." "Why they surely are human beings as well?"

RUDOLF HEINRICHSHOFEN   Schizophrenic; homemade book with colored drawings and texts, about 1919.

# ALOIS DALLMAYR

Dr. Mayer in the Educational = Home
Director Vocke
This little doctor pivots between 2 little birds!-
One screams clik and the other cluk.
Dr. Mayr's head is cured: costs 20 Marks Dr. Dallberger.
Information from Madame Senior Public Health Officer Dr. Vocker.
The policeman standing there sends greetings!

Information from vicar Simon.

Cunts <u>can be had</u> from the doorman of the Central Theater in the Rosen Lane.

<u>The Oeser family has been sworn in and vows death.</u>
<u>Eglfing</u> will consider this house <u>terror!</u>
Upper Bavarian Sanatorium Eglfing. Owner: <u>Alois Dallmayr</u>
<u>Police dog Oeser</u> sends greetings to the <u>esteemed management.</u>
On my behalf I am to send greetings from Madame head gardener <u>Oeser,</u> if you ever need draught draught-oxen, you can have them immediately.

Dallmayr has not <u>died out</u> for any friend or foe.

<u>No visiting privileges for time and eternity and my law is</u> <u>stronger than the power of the state.</u> I make so bold as to inform you, forced by my sacred advisory council matter, that the impressions of my faithful services have been bitten by a phony cat, and that my - earnest intention to release myself should serve as a warning to you in the best fashion of deception.

ALOIS DALLMAYR    Schizophrenic; pencil on paper, undated.


## JOHANNES FRIEDRICH

ESSAY ABOUT THE HORSE

The horse is a useful animal. It eats oats, bran and hay and drinks only pure water. There are riding horses military horses draught horses mountain horses. The draught horse is the poorest animal. I: have seen already so often that the drivers linger over wine and liquor or beer in the pubs in winter and in summer, and the horse just has to stand there in snow or frost when it is so cold in winter or when there is snow on the ground.

Or if it is summer, the horse must stand in that great heat until the drinker has been defeated by the devil alcohol, and the poor horse has to stay all that time in heat or rain or frost or snow The drivers give their horses the dry hay but no water because they are so lazy from alcohol the horses have the dry stuff and are thirsty and there is no water. Oh water; water; then the horse longs for his stall, when the drivers come out of the saloon drunk then the horses are beaten and chased until they are finally in their stable. The horse has a heart a lung guts liver kidneys two fore and hind legs bones flesh and beautiful hair. Its head consists of two eyes a nose a mouth. It has teeth in the mouth the teeth are attached to the jaws and between them is the tongue. On its legs it has four hooves there are horseshoes on the hooves. Heidelberg 15 May 1908

JOHANNES FRIEDRICH   Psychopath; sheet from school exercise note book with text and drawings, 1908.

## KARL A.

Schoenberg, Julye 16 1909

I undersigned at end remember exactly that as a little boy I took the juice of a hatched snake egg, because the mother snake was taking a bath in the nearby river and I used this moment to take an egg, the little eggs sat close together in a clump, and when I opened the egg, a small one slipped out, it happened in bright sunshine, and the little one was black or, rather, the young one fell to the ground, and the juice of the egg ran over my fingers which I licked with my tongue, the young one grew before my seeing eyes, turned snow-white from the sunrays, and I ran away and the little snake after me but couldn't catch me and I was happy that I luckily escaped, the juice tasted so sweet, and I was enchanted from that hour on, and I often had the wish to once more take the juice from such an egg but unfortunately I never had the chance, the juice had that ability it swelled my head and gave me such a handsome appearance which I would have liked to tell others, therefore I was and am the little enchanted Emperor's son Prince F.C.W. v. A.H. Ahrenottjberg secondly the juice has probably helped to keep a man's virility in the bones and was not lost, and I have drunk a lot of water with that until the sweet taste was gone

I ask that this letter be examined whether the man who has written this was ever crazy because I have to demand that
Sincerely

Prince Friedrich C.W. v. A.H. Ahrenottjberg

KARL A.   Schizophrenic; double sheet with text and drawing, 1909.

## KARL JOST

He hears: no voices.
He hears: a voice!
He hears voices! To your health! Karly!

Saloon The Sun.

Oh! Karly!
Sun-saloonkeeper: Karly! you
are going to be locked up!

KARL JOST   Delerium tremens; 1894.

Heidelberg, Oct. 24 1901
<u>Mental asylum</u> Oh you
sad word

Mrs. Rigassi, divorced Ahorn, snake and poisoner, murderess of her two boys. Responding to your simpleminded letter I am informing you that I am the son of God our marriage is divorced naturally only at table and bed, we will be married forever, but we will <u>not</u> see each other again in our entire life My Father (God) has told me that the children are not by me. You want to tell me now who the fathers of these children are I have suffered a terrible illness and have only my Father to thank that I am still alive I have been driven crazy from sorrow and worry. Farewell madame you are the meanest woman walking the earth A <u>great</u> <u>whore</u> I cannot satisfy you any more.

I remain your ruined husband and former spouse and husband fighting death

Ahorn

JULIUS AHORN    Paralysis; 1901.

# ERWIN STARRE

## TELEGRAM

(To) Starre (accent mark over e) Mannheim, Seckenheimerstr. 40
XII. 08
Unless been taken away from
here by tonight, will until
tomorrow as lunatic, upon most holy word of honor,
stare at the sun, or
bash in my temple with a post.
3 a 5 = 1.80 Marks. Either, or!
Erwin


## INSCRIPTION FOR MY GRAVESTONE!

> Teased by fate,
> Terrified by ill fortune,
> Stuck into a marriage,
> Died in the cesspool,
> The earth covers him.
> R.I.P.
> Easter 1918

TRANSLATOR'S NOTE:
Literal translation; the original rhymes.

ERWIN STARRE    Manic-depressive; 1908.

## COMPLAINTS

1.) A letter for Mr. Professor Willmanns has been intercepted, I had delivered it to the Professor's substitute.

2.) False complaints have been written about unrest and refusal to work, please, those persons, sisters, etc., who written false letters, in front of me in the presence of the Professor.

3.) Permission from the Professor himself, was refused, since the sisters made lying statements, that my paints and pencil are poisonous paints.

4.) The sisters demanded girls and women in on my name Reich, Lang, Seitz, and led these persons to the men's bedrooms, because I myself heard women's voices calling, you are not Reich, Lange, Seitz by a long shot, now they are taking us with force. Please, Your Grace, look among the women yourself, but quietly, because the so-called sisters sometimes hide girls and women without letting them visit Your Grace, many had asked for me, but all were refused a meeting with me, in order to never let me sleep one night with a woman, since I haven't ever from 1914 until today spent a night together upstairs with a woman, such rotten terrible impudence! for this reason they put me together upstairs with the prisoners, why do you refuse me writing paper. Insist on my correctly described complaints, will do court complaint because of this mistreatment. They don't even let animals wait that long, even animals cry, if they are separated that long, why did creator of the earth create humans and animals? to mistreat them? certainly not! Don't do unto others what you don't want done to you.

truthfully Reich, called Lang. Seitz

LORENZ SEITZ   Schizophrenic; 1921.

# THEODOR SCHWEBIG

Highly honored
Sovereign!
What can I write?
How can I express myself? Ah! Oh!
Please! Please! Please! Please!
Please! Please! Please! Please!
Please! Please! Please! Please!
Please! Please! Please! Please!
Please! Please! Please! Please!
Please! Please! Please! Please!
Please! Please! Please! Please!
Please! Please! Please! Please!
Please! Please! Please! Please!
Please! Please! Please! Please!
Please! Please! Please! Please!

Please, please highly honored Master and
King; I would like so much
to have a charity position.
With the best

Oh, please                              piety
forgive
that I have written                     Theodor Schwebig
with a pencil,
because it was done
in a case of emergency.

THEODOR SCHWEBIG    Catatonic; 1905.

**250**

Bachmann, Stephen, ed.
**Preach Liberty: Selections from the Bible for Progressives**
pb: $10.95

Beuys, Joseph.
**Energy Plan for the Western Man: Joseph Beuys in America**
cl: $18.95

David, Kati.
**A Child's War: WW II Through the Eyes of Children**
cl: $17.95

Dubuffet, Jean.
**Asphyxiating Culture and Other Writings**
cl: $17.95

Fried, Ronald K.
**Corner Men: Great Boxing Trainers**
cl: $21.95

Gould, Jay M., and Goldman, Benjamin.
**Deadly Deceit: Low-Level Radiation, High-Level Cover-up**
cl:$19.95, pb: $10.95

Hoffman, Abbie.
**The Best of Abbie Hoffman: Selections from "Revolution for the Hell of It," "Woodstock Nation", "Steal This Book" and new writings**
cl: $21.95, pb: $14.95

Howard-Howard, Margo (with Abbe Michaels).
**I Was a White Slave in Harlem**
pb: $12.95

Johnson, Phyllis, and Martin, David, eds.
**Frontline Southern Africa: Destructive Engagement**
cl: $23.95, pb: $14.95

Jones, E.P.
**Where Is Home? Living Through Foster Care**
cl: $17.95, pb: $9.95

Null, Gary.
**The Complete Guide to Sensible Eating**
pb:$14.95

Null, Gary, and Robins, Howard, D.P.M.
**How to Keep Your Feet and Legs Healthy for a Lifetime: The Complete Guide to Foot and Leg Care**
pb: $12.95

Ridgeway, James.
**Cast a Cold Eye: The Best Columns of 1990-91**
cl: $18.95, pb: $9.95

Ridgeway, James.
**The March to War**
pb: $10.95

Wasserman, Harvey.
**Harvey Wasserman's History of the United States**
pb: $8.95

Zerden, Sheldon.
**The Best of Health**
cl: $28.95, pb: $14.95

# Four Walls Eight Windows
# non-fiction

To order directly from the publisher, please complete the order form below and send with check or money order to:

Four Walls Eight Windows
PO Box 548, Village Station
New York, NY 10014
or Call 1-800-835-2246 (ext.123)
to order with an American Express® Card

| Qty. | Title | Price |
|---|---|---|
|  |  |  |
|  |  |  |
|  |  |  |
|  |  |  |
|  |  |  |

Name _____

Address (no PO Boxes) _____

City/State/Zip _____

| | |
|---|---|
| Subtotal | |
| Postage | $2.50 |
| TOTAL | |

Prices valid through 12/31/92.

☐ Send me a free catalogue

Algren, Nelson.
**The Man With The Golden Arm**
pb: $9.95
**Never Come Morning**
pb: $8.95
**The Neon Wilderness**
pb: $8.95

Anderson, Sherwood.
**The Triumph of the Egg**
pb: $8.95

Boetie, Dugmore.
**Familiarity Is the Kingdom of the Lost**
pb: $6.95

Brodsky, Michael.
**Dyad**
cl: $23.95, pb: $11.95
**Three Goat Songs**
cl: $18.95, pb: $9.95
**X in Paris**
pb: $9.95
**Xman**
cl: $21.95, pb: $11.95

Codrescu, Andrei, ed.
**American Poetry Since 1970 : Up Late**
2nd ed. cl: $25.95, pb: $14.95

Ernaux, Annie.
**A Woman's Story**
cl: $15.95

Grimes, Tom.
**A Stone of the Heart**
pb: $15.95

Kalberkamp, Peter.
**Mea Culpa**
pb: $10.95

Martin, Augustine, ed.
**Forgiveness: Ireland's Best Contemporary Short Stories**
cl: $25.95, pb: $12.95

Oakes, John G.H., ed.
**In the Realms of the Unreal: "Insane" Writings**
cl: $24.95, pb: $12.95

Perdue, Tito.
**Lee**
cl: $17.95

Rabon, Israel.
**The Street**
pb: $9.95

Rivera, Oswald.
**Fire and Rain**
pb: $17.95

Santos, Rosario, ed.
**And We Sold the Rain: Contemporary Fiction from Central America**
cl: $18.95, pb: $9.9.5

Sokolov, Sasha.
**A School for Fools**
pb: $9.95

Vassilikos, Vassilis.
**Z**
pb: $11.95